LIBRARIES
IN '90s
THE
What the Leaders Expect

LIBRARIES IN THE '90s

What the Leaders Expect

by Donald E. Riggs &
Gordon A. Sabine

Phoenix ◆ New York
ORYX PRESS
1988

The rare Arabian Oryx is believed to have inspired the myth of the unicorn. This desert antelope became virtually extinct in the early 1960s. At that time several groups of international conservationists arranged to have 9 animals sent to the Phoenix Zoo to be the nucleus of a captive breeding herd. Today the Oryx population is nearly 800, and over 400 have been returned to reserves in the Middle East.

Copyright © 1988 by
The Oryx Press
2214 North Central at Encanto
Phoenix, Arizona 85004-1483

Published simultaneously in Canada

∞ The paper used in this publication meets the minimum requirements of American National Standard for Information Science—Permanence of Paper for Printed Library Materials, ANSI Z39.48, 1984.

Library of Congress Cataloging-in-Publication Data

Riggs, Donald E.
  Libraries in the '90s.

  Includes index.
  1. Library science—Forecasting. 2. Libraries—
United States—Forecasting. 3. Librarians—United
States—Interviews. I. Sabine, Gordon A. II. Title.
Z665.R55 1988   020   88-20521
ISBN 0-89774-532-9

Contents

——— ◆ ◆ ◆ ———

Preface

———— ♦ ♦ ♦ ————

The idea for this book came from a book written by Guy Lyle, long-time and highly respected librarian at Emory University. In the late 1960s, he interviewed 16 college and university librarians and made their remarks into *The Librarian Speaking: Interviews with University Librarians* (University of Georgia Press, Athens, 1970).

This time around, we have included all types of librarians— academic, public, school, state, and special, plus library school deans. Also included are three very important nationally known individuals who have had great impact upon the library community over the nation and indeed the world.

In his preface, Lyle justified his study because of "the conviction or suspicion that university librarianship is . . . reaching a turning point in its history." And he continued:

> At the moment technology is one of the compelling forces constantly shaping librarianship. At the same time specialization proliferates. The library is viewed as one element in a complex communication system and the pressure is on librarians to produce faster and better ways of acquiring, organizing and retrieving information. . . It will take some time for the technological yearning and learning that is being churned up in library journals, library institutes, and library conventions to change into action. When this happens library aims and services will probably be altered to a degree which will make them unrecognizable. . . .

So here we are, almost 20 years later. Lyle fairly predicted much of our world today. (Of course, there have been other changes too; just one of his 16 interviewees was a woman—but 12 of our 25 interviewees happen to be.)

This volume has two parts. The afterword is a presentation of the challenges and opportunities facing librarians in the 1990s. Don Riggs wrote it and also chose the interviewees.

Chapters 1-16 are the edited versions of the face-to-face tape-recorded interviews held with the contributing authors, mostly at the 1988 San Antonio midwinter ALA conference, but sometimes in the interviewees' offices. In a few cases, the initial interviews were augmented by follow-up telephone calls. Gordon Sabine conducted and edited the interviews.

In all cases, interviewees have read and approved the published copy.

There was not just one uniform question schedule. Rather, topics were adapted to individuals and their special expertise. You will read answers from almost everyone to a few of the queries but also the answers from only one or two interviewees to other, more specialized, questions.

Before you proceed, we strongly suggest that you read the biographical profiles of the contributors so that you can relate answers with a particular kind of library experience and assignment. And one reminder: These were *oral* interviews. What you'll read is conversational dialog, not a formal manuscript intended for a formal research journal. Understandably, the language and the sentence structure will be relaxed and informal.

The debt both you and we owe to the interviewees is great. Their advice and projections, always thoughtful, sometimes varied and even contradictory, are the ingredients to make our future easier than our past, if only we will heed.

♦ ♦ ♦

Two threads run through the thoughts of the library leaders in this book. One says that to be of the greatest use to the greatest number in the future, librarians must comprehend, then conquer, the complexities of technology and automation in their workplace. The other asserts that to be of greatest service and have the greatest impact in the future, librarians must be "people" people, providing personalized, individualized, one-on-one, human-being-to-human-being responses. And that leads us to wonder: Are the two separate or perhaps connected? Could it be that the first actually brought on the need for the second? Must an aware librarian be in just one camp or another? Or are the very best really going to be at ease in both?

If what follows starts you thinking along these lines, then forging your own answers, our purpose will have been fulfilled.

♦ ♦ ♦

The book would not have been possible without the cooperation-beyond-the-call-of-duty from each contributor, plus the work of Bette Baldwin and Vanessa Keys in the Arizona State University Library, and that in the Oryx Press of the always cheerful and supportive (which is what an assistant to the publisher should be) Dick DeBacher, and the always questioning but not querulous (which is what a good editor also should be) Jan Krygier.

Donald E. Riggs
Gordon A. Sabine

The Contributors

Asp ♦ Berger ♦ Chisholm ♦ Cooper ♦ De Gennaro ♦
Dougherty ♦ Dumont ♦ Eastman ♦ Farber ♦ Goral ♦ Heim ♦
Kilgour ♦ Mason ♦ McDonald ♦ Owens ♦ Rosenthal ♦ Smith
♦ Stepanian ♦ Strong ♦ Summers ♦ Vasilakis ♦ Wedgeworth
♦ Welsh ♦ Whitney ♦ Wisener ♦ Riggs ♦ Sabine

──── ♦ ♦ ♦ ────

 WILLIAM ASP has been director, Office of
Library Development and Services, Minne-
sota Department of Education, since 1975.
He has a B.A. in history and an M.L.S.
from the University of Minnesota. He was
director of the East Central Regional Library, Cambridge, MN, and taught at the
University of Iowa School of Library Science. He is an ALA councilor at large and
has been chair of the Chief Officers of State
Library Agencies, chair of the White House
Conference on Library and Information
Services (WHCLIS) Task Force, founder and board member of the
Minnesota Library Foundation, chair of the Minnesota Adult Literacy Campaign Coalition, and board member of Library Resources, Inc. He was Minnesota librarian of the year, 1982, and
received the WHCLIS special award in 1984.

PATRICIA WILSON BERGER is a candidate for the position of 1988–89 American Library Association president-elect and, since 1983, has been chief, Information Resources and Services Division, National Bureau of Standards. She has a B.A. from George Washington University and an M.L.S. from the Catholic University of America. She has worked at American University, Johns Hopkins University, the Institute for Defense Analysis, the Commission on Government Procurement, the U.S. Patent and Trademark Office, and the Environmental Protection Agency. She has been an ALA councilor at large and is a governor-appointed member of the Library Board of Virginia, past president of the Washington, D.C., chapter of the Special Library Association, and a 1987 SLA Fellow. She has won Outstanding Administrative Management awards from the U.S. Department of Commerce, and the Federal Librarians Round Table achievement award.

MARGARET CHISHOLM is 1987–88 president, American Library Association and, since 1981, has been professor and director, Graduate School of Library and Information Sciences, University of Washington. She has B.A., M.L.S., and Ph.D. degrees from the University of Washington. She has taught at the Universities of Oregon and New Mexico and has been professor and dean, College of Library and Information Services, University of Maryland and vice-president for University Relations and Development, University of Washington. A prolific author, lecturer, and consultant, she has been chair, Council of Deans and Directors, American Library and Information Science Educators, and is a trustee-at-large for the National Association of Public Television Stations. She has won the outstanding alumna award from both St. Cloud University and the University of Washington.

BARBARA D. COOPER is public affairs director, Omni, Inc., of Fort Lauderdale, FL, and past president, American Library Trustees Association. She attended San Jose State College and has been an ALA council member; chair of the ALTA White House Conference implementation subcommittee; member and chair, Broward County Library Advisory Board and Library Foundation; secretary, Council for Florida Libraries, Inc.; member and vice-chair, Florida State Library advisory council; member and past chair, WHCLIS; chair, both Florida and Southeastern Library associations Trustees and Friends; and chair, Governor's White House Conference Steering Committee. She has received both Florida Library Association and American Library Association Trustees and Friends citations.

RICHARD De GENNARO is director, New York Public Library. He has a B.A. in government, an M.A. in liberal studies from Wesleyan University, Middleton, CT, an M.S.L. from Columbia University, and is a graduate of the Harvard Business School Advanced Management program. From 1970–86, he was Director of Libraries and adjunct professor of English at the University of Pennsylvania, and from 1958–70, he worked in various positions in the Harvard University Library, attaining the rank of senior associate university librarian. He started library work in the New York Public Library in 1956 as a reference librarian. A prolific author and consultant and member of editorial and publication boards, he has been president, Association of Research Libraries. He received the 1986 ALA Melvil Dewey award, a Council on Library Resources fellowship, and first place in the *American Libraries* prize article competition.

RICHARD M. DOUGHERTY was for 10 years from 1978 director, University Library and Professor of Information and Library Studies, University of Michigan. In the summer of 1988, he resigned his library post and turned to full-time teaching and research. He holds a B.S. in forestry from Purdue, and an M.L.S. and Ph.D. from Rutgers. He has taught at Rutgers, University of North Carolina–Chapel Hill, University of Southern California, University of Wisconsin–Madison, Syracuse, Baylor, the University of California–Berkeley, and Aberyswyth, Wales. He has been acquisitions head, University of North Carolina–Chapel Hill Libraries; associate director of libraries, University of Colorado; and university librarian, University of California–Berkeley. He is co-founder and editor of the *Journal of Academic Librarianship* and *Library Issues*. He was ACRL academic/research librarian of the year and a Rutgers distinguished alumnus.

PAUL E. DUMONT has been, since 1976, director of technical services at the seven-campus Dallas County (TX) Community College district. He holds a B.A. in economics from St. Francis College and an M.L.S. from the Catholic University of America. He has been systems librarian at San Antonio College and chief of materials processing services at the Dallas Public Library. He has been chair of the college and university division of the Texas Library Association, president of the Texas chapter of the Association of College and Research Libraries, and president of the Dallas Chapter of the Association of Records Managers and Administrators, from which he received the 1984 chapter Member of the Year award. He directed the installation in Dallas of two automated library systems: ALIS (in 1977) and NOTIS (in 1987) for the district colleges' learning resources center.

ANN HEIDBREDER EASTMAN is public affairs officer, University Libraries, and university faculty book publishing staff officer, Virginia Tech. She earned a B.A. in English at the University of Michigan. In New York City, she worked in the school and library field for major publishers; was senior associate for education and library services, Association of American Publishers; research director, National Book Committee; and assistant director for national programs, National Library Week. She was director of admissions, Chatham College, Pittsburgh, PA. She has been a member of the ALA council; past president, Library Administration and Management Association; executive committee member, Center for the Book, Library of Congress; past president, Women's National Book Association; and citizen delegate to WHCLIS from Virginia. She won the 1986 Women's National Book Association award.

EVAN I. FARBER has been, since 1962, librarian, Earlham College, Richmond, IN. He has a B.A. and an M.A. in political science and a B.S. in library science from the University of North Carolina–Chapel Hill. He was librarian at the State Teachers College, Livingston, AL, and chief, serials and binding division, Emory University Library. He has been a prolific author, editor, consultant, speaker, and workshop leader; ALA council member; president, Association of College and Research Libraries; advisory board member, Indiana University School of Library and Information Science; and member of the OCLC advisory committee of academic and university libraries. He received an honorary DHL from St. Lawrence University and was named ACRL academic/research librarian of the year 1980, and bibliographic instruction librarian of the year 1987.

BARBARA J. GORAL has been, since 1985, director, Colorado State Library for the Blind and Physically Handicapped. She has a B.S. from Western Michigan University and an M.L.S. from Wayne State University. She has been corporate librarian for Michigan Blue Cross and Blue Shield, head of reference and cataloging at the Wayne Oakland Library Federation, and assistant director and director of the Wayne County Regional Library for the Blind and Physically Handicapped. She is one of six members of the Colorado State Library's Management Team, which advises the state librarian on policy and procedure. She was chair of the Midlands Conference of Librarians for the Blind and Physically Handicapped and will serve in that post again for the group's 1988–89 Western Conference.

KATHLEEN HEIM is dean and professor, Louisiana State University School of Library and Information Science. She has a B.A. in English from the University of Illinois at Chicago, an M.A. in English from Marquette University, an M.L.S. from the University of Chicago, and a Ph.D. in library and information science from the University of Wisconsin–Madison. She has worked on the library staffs at Elmhurst and Rosary Colleges and taught at Triton College, the University of Wisconsin–Madison, and the University of Illinois. A prolific writer and speaker, she is editor of *RQ*, past president of the Association for Library and Information Science Education, and member of the Louisiana Governor's Commission for Women. She won the 1987 ALA Equality award for "promoting equality in the information profession."

FREDERICK KILGOUR has been, since 1967, the founder, president, and executive director of the Ohio College Library Center and developer of the Online Computer Library Center, which serves thousands of libraries in the U.S. and 19 foreign nations. He holds a B.A. from Harvard. He has been editor of the *Journal of Library Automation* and managing editor of the *Yale Journal of Biology and Medicine*. He started work in the Harvard College Library as an undergraduate, served in the Office of Strategic Services during World War II, and was lecturer and librarian of the Yale Medical Library before moving to Ohio. He has been awarded the Legion of Merit; was named Ohio librarian of the year; received the Margaret Mann citation, the Melvil Dewey medal, and the Marcia Noyes award of the Medical Library Association; was named academic/research librarian of the year; and has received honorary degrees from Marietta (OH) College, Ohio State University, Wooster (OH) College, and Denison University. His latest project is EIDOS (Electronic Information Delivery Online System). EIDOS will initially allow users, via terminals, to access information directly from books and journals.

MARILYN GELL MASON has been, since 1986, director, Cleveland Public Library. She has a B.A. from the University of Dallas, an M.L.S. from North Texas State University, and an M.P.A. degree from Harvard. She was director of the Atlanta-Fulton Public Library from 1982 to 1986. She has served as director of the 1979–80 White House Conference on Library and Information Science (WHCLIS); executive vice-president of Metrics Research Corporation; chief of library programs, Washington Metropolitan Council of Governments; and has held various positions in the Dallas and San Antonio public libraries, NTSU library, New Jersey State Library, and the Arlington County Department of Libraries. She is a member, OCLC board of directors, and has received the Presidential Award of Appreciation, the first distinguished alumna award of the NTSU library school, and delivered the Kennedy School commencement address at Harvard.

MARILYN M. McDONALD has been, since 1984, dean of learning resources, Foothill Community College, and director of its Library Technical Assistant program. She holds a B.A. and M.A. in economics from Stanford, an M.L.S. from San Jose State, and an M.B.A. from Golden Gate University, San Francisco, CA. She has been a research librarian at the National Bureau of Economic Research, Stanford; librarian for the San Jose and Palo Alto Unified School districts; and head of technical services for the Stanford Research Institute, International. She has been president of the technical services chapter of the California Library Association. She was a nominee for the Foothill Community College Innovator of the Year award in both 1985 and 1986.

MAJOR R. OWENS is the only professional librarian in the U.S. Congress. Since 1982 he has served in the House of Representatives for the 12th Congressional District, Brooklyn, NY. He has a B.A. degree from Morehouse College, Atlanta, GA, and an M.L.S. from Atlanta University. He has held various positions, including Community Coordinator with the Brooklyn Public Library, and was an adjunct professor of library science and director of the Community Media Program at Columbia University. He was keynote speaker at the 1979 WHCLIS. He was chair of the Brooklyn Congress of Racial Equality and vice-president of the Metropolitan Council on Housing, and was elected to the New York State Senate. He is a member of the House Governmental Operations committee, a senior member of its Education and Labor committee, chair of the subcommittee on Select Education, and chair of the Congressional Black Caucus Education Braintrust. He holds an honorary Doctor of Laws degree from Atlanta University.

JOSEPH A. ROSENTHAL has been, since 1979, university librarian at the University of California–Berkeley. He holds a B.A. in political science from Dickinson College, Carlisle, PA, an M.A. in political science from Pennsylvania State University, and an M.L.S. from Columbia University. He worked as reference and documents librarian and as chief, preparation services, New York Public Library, and has been with the Berkeley library since 1971. He has taught at both the Columbia and Berkeley library schools. He is a member of the Association of College and Research Libraries legislation committee, has been president of the Information Science and Automation division, and has served on the board of directors for both the New York Technical Services Librarians and the Center for Research Libraries, and as an ALA councilor at large.

ELIZABETH MARTINEZ SMITH has been, since 1979, librarian, Orange County Public Library, Orange, CA. She holds a B.A. in Latin American Studies from the University of California–Los Angeles and an M.L.S. from the University of Southern California. For the Los Angeles County Public Library she has been children's librarian, field coordinator, special services consultant, and principal librarian for service to institutions. She has taught at the California State University (Fullerton) School of Library Science, was a delegate to the 1979 WHCLIS, founded the ALA Chicano Task Force, and is a trustee of the California State Summer School for the Arts. She was co-editor of the *Wilson Library Bulletin* issue on library service to the Spanish speaking, and won the 1982 Hispanic Women's Recognition award from the League of Latin American Citizens.

ELLEN M. STEPANIAN has been, since 1972, director of library media, Shaker Heights City School District, Shaker Heights, OH. She holds a B.S. from Syracuse University, an M.A. from Teachers College, Columbia University, and an M.L.S. from Rosary College. A prolific speaker and workshop presenter, she is chair of the organizational and evaluation committee of the American Association of School Librarians; board member for the Association for Library Service to Children; and is on the editorial and advisory board, Library Administration and Management Association. She is vice-president of the OHIONET trustees, on the Bowker Library advisory board, and member, advisory council, Kent State University School of Library Science. She won the 1982 AASL Media Program of the Year award and received the 1984 Award of Merit of the Ohio Educational Library Media Association.

GARY E. STRONG is state librarian of California. He holds a B.S. from the University of Idaho and an M.L.S. from the University of Michigan. He has been deputy state librarian for the Washington State Library, public library director in the Everett (WA) and Lake Oswego (OR) public libraries, and extension librarian in Moscow, ID. He has been president of the Chief Officers of State Library Agencies, Library Administration and Management Association, Pacific Northwest Library, and Oregon Library associations. He is chief executive officer of the California Library Services Board, executive director and member of the Board of Directors of the California State Library Foundation, and editor of the *California State Library Foundation Bulletin*. In 1984 he was named distinguished alumnus of the University of Michigan School of Library Science.

WILLIAM SUMMERS is 1988–89 ALA president and, since 1985, has been dean and professor at the Florida State University School of Library and Information Studies. He earned a B.A. from Florida State and an M.L.S. and Ph.D. from Rutgers. He has served on the staff of libraries in Jacksonville, FL; Linden, NJ; Cocoa, FL; and Providence, RI; and was Florida state librarian. He taught at the University of South Carolina College of Library and Information Science, and from 1976–85 was its dean. He has been in ALA leadership positions since 1972. He also has been president of the Association of American Library Schools and of both the Rhode Island and South Carolina Library associations. Rutgers named him its 1987 School of Communication, Library and Information Studies distinguished alumnus.

MARY VASILAKIS is manager, Information and Communication Services, Westinghouse Electric Corporation, Nuclear Energy Systems, Pittsburgh, PA. She holds a B.S. in biological sciences from the University of Pittsburgh and an M.L.S. from Duquesne University. In the Special Library Association, she has been chair, Pittsburgh chapter; national chair, nuclear science and public utilities divisions; and member and secretary, board of directors. She has taught at the Pittsburgh Graduate School of Library and Information Science. She was a member of the Pennsylvania state delegation, WHCLIS. She received the Westinghouse Award of Merit in 1977 and was named to the first group of SLA Fellow Members in 1987.

ROBERT WEDGEWORTH has been, since 1985, dean, School of Library Service, Columbia University. For 13 years he was ALA executive director. He holds an A.B. in English literature from Wabash College and an M.L.S. from the University of Illinois–Urbana. He has been a cataloger, Kansas City Public Library; acting librarian, Park College; librarian, Meramec Community College; assistant librarian, Brown University; and assistant professor, Library and Information Science, Rutgers. He is president of the National Association of Wabash Men. He has been trustee or member or advisor to the Library of Congress, Newberry Library, the U.S. Information Agency, the American Library in Paris, and the International Federation of Library Associations and Institutions, The Hague. Park College, Wabash College, Atlanta University, Western Illinois University, and The College of William and Mary have awarded him honorary degrees.

WILLIAM J. WELSH has been Deputy Librarian of Congress since 1976. He holds an A.B. from Notre Dame. He has been at the Library of Congress since 1947. He served in the U.S. Air Force, 1941–47, as librarian for the Alaskan division headquarters of the Air Transport Command. He is a prolific author, speaker, and library consultant. He is a member, American Friends of the Vatican Library advisory board; Massachusetts Institute of Technology visiting committee for libraries; Association of Research Libraries task force on National Library Network Development; and chair, Conference of Directors of National Libraries. He received the ALA Melvil Dewey award in 1971, the Library of Congress Distinguished Service award for his leadership in the areas of preservation and uses of new technologies in 1983, and an honorary Doctor of Laws from Notre Dame in 1984.

KAREN WHITNEY has been library director at Agua Fria Union High School, Glendale, AZ, since 1979. She was the 1987–88 president of the American Association of School Librarians. She holds a B.S. in education and an M.L.S. from the University of Oklahoma. She also has served as librarian for the Arizona Department of Corrections and Alhambra High School, and was library media department chair, North High School, Phoenix, AZ. In the Arizona State Library Association, she was school library division president, conference program chair, executive board member, and 1986–87 president. In the AASL, she has been affiliate assembly chair, secretary, and Minneapolis conference co-chair. She was named Arizona librarian of the year, 1983.

JOANNE WISENER is a trustee and has been president of the Yuma, AZ, city-county library board and is former president and committee chair of the American Library Trustees Association. She has a B.S. in education from Stanford and taught 20 years in California and Arizona schools. She is a member of the Arizona State Advisory Council on Libraries, co-chair of the Friends/Trustees Roundtable, Arizona State Library Association, and past president of the Arizona Library Friends. She has received the Madora Ingalls library service award from the Yuma Library Council, the ASLA Rosenzweig award, an ALA trustee citation, and a State of Arizona legislative commendation.

DONALD E. RIGGS is dean of the Arizona State University libraries, which he has headed since 1979. His education includes a B.A. in biological science from Glenville State College, Glenville, WV; an M.A. in liberal arts and administration from West Virginia University; an M.L.S. from the University of Pittsburgh; and an Ed.D. from Virginia Polytechnic Institute and State University. He has served as an academic library director for 18 years. Prior to going to Arizona State University, he was director of libraries for the University of Colorado at Denver; Metropolitan State College, Denver; and Community College of Denver–Auraria Campus. He has taught information science at the University of Colorado and library management at the University of Arizona. Author of numerous articles and books, he is editor of *Library Administration and Management* and serves on the *Journal of Library Administration* Editorial Board. He has served in various ALA offices, as president of three state library associations, as a trustee of public libraries, and as a consultant for all types of libraries.

GORDON A. SABINE is special assistant for oral history to the dean of university libraries at Arizona State University. He has a B.A. and M.A. in journalism and economics from the University of Wisconsin–Madison and a Ph.D. in political science from the University of Minnesota. A reporter and editor for newspapers, magazines, and United Press, he has taught journalism and was dean of the University of Oregon School of Journalism, founding dean of the College of Communications Arts and vice-president for special projects at Michigan State University, director of the University of Iowa School of Journalism, and founding professor of the journalism curriculum at Virginia Tech. He won Carnegie Corporation young administrator and American College Testing program senior research fellowships, and was a professor-in-residence at Time, Inc.

LIBRARIES IN THE '90s

What the Leaders Expect

Chapter 1

New Services

In this chapter, more than half the interviewees look into the future and predict changes in library services that both librarians and users will find during the next 10 years. You'll understand their answers better if you've read the preceding "Contributors" section and can link each interviewee with his or her career experience, orientation, and current assignment. Other questions addressed here: What is the dividing line on charging fees? At what stage do you start charging for what kinds of things? Preservation: Why has there been so much talk but so little action? What's needed to get the ball really rolling?

———— ♦ ♦ ♦ ————

What new library services do you anticipate in the next 10 years?

WHITNEY: School librarians are going to become much more actively involved with teachers in the instructional process. In the past, school libraries have been considered a support service. That's changing. Activities that take place in a school library are perfect for teaching students to begin to think creatively and critically, and that is being recognized more and more.

And I see more teachers participating in the design of instruction and in the use of a variety of resources, rather than reliance upon a single textbook with an occasional film added just for spice. I see the resources of the library media program becoming really the basis for learning.

As for how a school librarian gets more involved with the instructional process, there's no simple answer. The key is establishing a relationship with the teaching faculty. To develop a partnership means that you have to be willing to share. You have to be willing to make a mistake. You can't be frightened at letting someone see that you tried something and it didn't work. You have to have the confidence to fail. And I think maybe that's one of the biggest challenges we have.

Many times the teachers don't want anyone to know what's happening in their own classrooms. They really prefer to go in and shut the door and then if something doesn't work, nobody knows but them. And to open that door and let someone else interact with you and see when something doesn't work takes a person who has a lot of self-confidence.

The teacher is not likely to come to the librarian asking for this help. It's incumbent upon us to get out there and let people know what we can do and that we're willing to start the process.

BERGER: Home-grown databases should be commonplace. I think you will find in medium-sized and large special libraries a number of databases being created and maintained for the organization, or for perhaps a whole network of organizations.

Special libraries in the past have tended to network very heavily, but among themselves. They have not been particularly willing or anxious to share their expertise and resources with other kinds of libraries and institutions.

That is changing, and of course one of the reasons it is changing is because of the creation and the development of facilities like OCLC. While special library services will continue to be somewhat different, the distinctions we have known in the past among the various kinds of libraries in this country will tend to disappear.

It's going to be increasingly difficult to point at a library and say that it is strictly an academic library because I think you're going to see a lot of specialized services created in that academic environment which simply aren't there now, or not in great numbers, and certainly not well known.

McDONALD: We'll have more full-text retrieval of periodicals than we do now. We certainly have the potential to do that now, and we don't have storage space for a large periodical collection. I certainly see reference books and books like encyclopedias and dictionaries using the electronic format, particularly laser technology. Librarians will increase their expertise in online information retrieval.

GORAL: More material. Because of the format that we use, we are producing very little material for the blind and handicapped or the print impaired. This group is better educated and is getting older. They are requiring more specialized information, and we just can't meet that with the materials we have right now.

VASILAKIS: We're heading in the direction right now where people won't find it necessary to come to the library. The library will be accessible to them through terminals in their own homes or offices.

The library's approach will be to make sure the right kinds of databases and the right kinds of information are in a central place where they can then be accessed.

The whole attitude of the library will be different. Now you're geared to the person who walks in, or the person who calls up, or the person who sends a FAX. In the future, you'll have to gear up to the person who will just hook in and see your collection on the PC. You've got to make your services available electronically; that's where the future is. I see technology changing the entire thrust of the library.

In industry especially there is a lot of pressure to ask what value you bring to the organization. We always had to be accountable but not to the degree that we're accountable today. So it's up to the library and the librarian to make sure we can justify value added to the organization. That is the key phrase today: to add value.

Value is measured by how you can help sell the product or how you can help the organization meet its commitment to the customer. The customer is the key. Our customers are the internal people we serve; they in turn serve the external customer. We're measured by how well we can serve the next person in line and then how well he or she can, in turn, serve that external customer.

If we can get the right information to people who invent things, who patent things, and they in turn can build a better generator for the utility customer, then we are adding value. If we can find the proper use of a metal or if through good use of census statistics, we can help find a market somewhere that hadn't been thought of, then we prove our worth and justify our expenses.

For example, when I was directly involved in the library I did some laborious searching through indexes and found that the date of a publication in a foreign country was such that our patent department was able to file a patent infringement suit. That suit saved the company a lot of money.

The librarian, like every employee of any company, has to remember that the business of business is to make a profit. The librarian has to provide services that help to do that.

The people who like libraries as we know them today are going to end up being archivists. In the corporate world, libraries won't exist as they exist today.

Do you realize the cost of one square foot of space and storage in the average library? That's why I think all the wonderful technologies that are coming down the pike for storing information, from the optical disks and the CD-ROM to even the holographic techniques, are so vital. They are going to provide a way to save space, and saving space means saving money.

Everyone's on PCs these days. You see people on airplanes working with their lap-top computers. The kids are getting these things in grade school. The whole world is changing as far as how people get information. Like it or not, librarians in corporations have to get out of the traditional library business and into the information business if they expect to survive.

In our library at Westinghouse, we now have 6,000 square feet. Our space requirements will change drastically. Everyone's going to have a sort of control room. People will have to be able to do what they do today, but just do it in front of a terminal. We won't have to store books anymore, but they'll all be accessible. I remember when *Chemical Abstracts* used to be rooms and rooms and rooms of stuff and today they are online.

We are in the testing stage of a system where our clientele can just peruse our card catalog on their PC. We've automated to that point. All they do is a key-word access, title or author, on an electronic request form. We don't even see them. We have some users who really enjoy doing it that way. Others, the older ones like me, like to come and browse.

One of the hardest things I ever had to do was throw out a card catalog. I ran two systems for about three years and finally I had to throw out the card catalog. It was tough to do, but we didn't need it anymore. We had a computer-generated printed book catalog and from that we now have an online catalog.

De GENNARO: By that time there should be a functioning telefacsimile within the library which connects us to other libraries throughout the country via RLIN and OCLC, and possibly other networks as well. Telefacsimile is a technology whose time has finally arrived. It has been predicted for the last 20 years, but it's one of those revolutions that never happened, that kept getting postponed.

I think that in general this library and others will be providing more extramural services through technology. My vision of the future is that we are going to expand our capabilities through technology to provide services beyond the library, to make the resources of the library available outside the library's walls.

I would like to see the NYPL expanding its capability to provide services all over the country and, indeed, all over the world through the technology.

We have already seen some of the effects that technology has had. Through the library networks, OCLC and RLIN, we facilitated the requesting of interlibrary loans; those requests are now pretty much instantaneous. The next step is to speed up the delivery of the material. That still takes too much time.

I can see us going more into providing to users, through branch libraries, information about jobs, about social services, information that people are going to need to help them get on with their lives. This means going beyond some of the traditional library services for recreation and for education.

And we're also coming to a point where the library's role will be to help people find what kind of training for jobs is available, what kind of organizations are available to help people to find out about these questions. A good deal of that is already going on, and by 1998 we'll be doing more of it, and it will become a more important part of our function.

NYPL already has a community information services directory, a directory of thousands of organizations that provide a wide variety of services to people. We are expanding it and we will be putting it online.

There's another kind of library service, the whole area of visual media, and especially cassettes. I read recently that there are already 50 million video cassette players in the homes in the U.S. In the next 10 years, we are going to be providing much more service in the visual media.

I'm not sure when and how we'll get into the business of providing library service via cable networks. Like telefacsimile, that's been one of those revolutions that has been promised over the years but has never been delivered. Its time may come, too.

I see more possibilities in cassettes than in cable. The Kellogg Foundation is funding a project to make a large number of educational and cultural programs that appear on the PBS available at a very low price to libraries for showings. I hope this is just the beginning.

DUMONT: The use of artificial intelligence will allow us to do Boolean key-word searching. It will allow us to gain access via a lot of different points to the same information.

We've been striving for integration of systems for many years. I see us finally coming to the point where these sub-systems either communicate with each other or are indeed assimilated. I see a confluence of these technologies interacting in unison.

The ability to take other types of databases and make them available to faculty and staff will really be the key. That is, to make it possible for scientists to gain access to machine-readable databases of things of interest to them in their profession through one work station and be able to gain access to the documents or data quickly. They will no longer have to interact with the librarian to gain access to this information through interlibrary loan somewhere. That's going to be a breakthrough for us as libraries and information centers.

FARBER: Not anything particularly new except a different kind of service. The reference function in the future, particularly in academic libraries, will be somewhat like a reader's advisor. The basic questions will be mostly answered by technology, particularly by expert systems, other forms of computer-assisted instruction, artificial intelligence.

Librarians will act much more as individual reference librarians, helping people evaluate their searches, shape their searches. They will act, in a sense, much more as information advisors for individuals and let the technology do the searching for the information.

ROSENTHAL: New perhaps is a little bit extreme. I see the changes in library operations and services as evolutionary, and extensions and modifications mostly of what we're already doing rather than dramatically new services.

One of the trends that I anticipate is that libraries and the people who work in them will be in a sort of extended—how do you say middle man without being chauvinistic?—middle man position as far as their users are concerned. That is, the librarians will advise scholars, particularly people who are doing advanced research, on what the best sources of information are, what the best formats are, what the most economical means are, for the scholar's purpose.

Librarians will become more like special librarians. They will deal more in information and less in simply saying, "Here's the bibliographic apparatus; it's up to you to find out which things you want." In certain situations, they may come to function more as part of a research team.

Since we'll be dealing more and more extensively in information—bibliographic and textual and numeric that's in electronic form—life is not going to get simpler. The world of information in electronic form is going to become very complicated because it will consist of concentric circles or spheres in which the scholar and the librarian operate. And in the space of 10 years I don't think the connections are going to become as smooth as we would like to envision.

There will be different protocols for accessing data in these different spheres or circles, and librarians will be kept busy trying to translate those protocols into simpler language for the researcher and trying to train people to use, to access, these different spheres of information.

The better librarians are at doing this, the more their services are going to be in demand. So to the extent that we and our successors are good, we will be building demand for our services. I think that's essential to do or else librarians and libraries will be sort of museums of information and not very heavily used.

STRONG: A lot of what I will respond to now comes from being, for eight years, the California state librarian, and California is a different world in so many ways.

One out of every ten people living in the United States today lives in California. We have a population that is more unlike any nation, from an ethnic and cultural point of view, than any other place on earth. We have an out-migration of Whites and an in-migration of refugees and people from South and Latin America, Central America, Southeast Asia.

The problems that we face from a library services standpoint are just incredible. We have some of the most prestigious research institutions in the world ranging from Rand Corporation to TRW, to SRI, to the University of California, Stanford University, USC, Pepperdine, and on and on. This gives us a wealth of riches, but it also gives us a very different kind of challenge when you consider what services should look like down the road.

This year, for the first year ever, the reference questions answered by the Los Angeles County Public Library exceeded the circulation out of that library. We predicted that trend in 1979 in our first Information Need Studies of Californians by the state library, which showed us some trends in increased demand for information from libraries as compared to television, radio, priests, ministers, neighbors.

We conducted that study again in 1985, and discovered that the incidence at which libraries were used as sources of information had increased tremendously. That began to tell us something was different.

We'd also come through Proposition 13, probably one of the most belt-tightening nightmares that any state has gone through. It's been replicated in a number of places, but I don't think it's been played out quite to the extent that we have in California, coupled with a revenue limitation measure that's just beginning to haunt us. In that process, libraries have had to look very hard at some things.

What did we lose? Take public libraries alone. We lost about a thousand staff FTE, about 10% of our staff. We lost 11% of the availability, open hours. We lost 25% of the buying power for materials. We spent every second in the next 10 years trying to recover those losses. Circulation has never gotten back to the level it had prior to Prop 13.

On the other hand, there's a better quality of service out there and it's much more available. The availability of materials in various formats is certainly there. Our public library systems are more in place.

We're going to see one of two scenarios in the next 10 years. One of them would say shut down access. Who's going to be able to get the information, regardless of what the format is? And we'll respond to the format as the marketplace determines. I don't think we determine that in libraries, necessarily. We're not enough of the market share. We also don't know what AT&T's doing in the next six months, which scares me.

It will boil down to access. It's going to get locked up and local communities are going to say, local universities are going to say, corporate headquarters are going to say, schools already have said, "we're going to hang on to what we've got and nobody can touch it but us."

Or we're going to continue to build on the open access features that we've had in our libraries. We're going to have more availability, we're going to have more access to whatever the formats are, even in the home, to what information we're able to pull together with public funds.

Through the interlibrary loan and direct loan programs of the California Library Service Act, we already allow a citizen to go to any public library in the state, and about 10% of the 125 million loans are made out of jurisdictions directly to a citizen without him or her having to worry about the jurisdictional limits of library structure. Individuals go in, they want something, they're treated like local patrons.

Behind the scenes we juggle the net imbalances and pay that local government. We don't pay the library, we pay the local government for providing that service outside its jurisdiction. And in turn, we expect them to have the collection open, the services available, on the same basis to nonresidents as they do to their residents.

In my arena with public policy decision making, time is the most crucial issue, and if during the legislative session my staff can't put something in a senior staff policy researcher staff member's hands in a couple of hours, it's worthless.

Let me give you a specific example. Handling confidentiality is really important because the state library works with all sides of the fence. The opposition wants us to research all of the news articles on a certain nominee for the last five years. Nine hundred citations are found and must be copied within 24 hours for their policy analysis.

Now the typical librarian would say, well, tell them to come over and copy the things. Not when I'm director of that library. We keep people on all night photocopying to put the articles in their hands so that they can do the analysis the very next morning.

With technology we can do much better collection development. In our statewide database program we can now analyze at the subject heading level, at the LC class level, by library.

For English-language materials, for example, we can overlay for the first time where that population is in the state and where the collections are. We can identify the gaps between where the people are and where the collections are. That's one of the beauties of some of the technology, how it allows us to manage collections.

When the cuts came in the state budget, I didn't cut my acquisitions budget. When I needed to automate, I did not raid the acquisitions budget to buy terminals and to buy systems. With a lot of my colleagues, the first thing they let go is the collection budget, and when they've got to automate and do retrospective conversion, they raid and don't buy. But the collection we will build and preserve—that's what's going to be there after all the rest of us are gone and there's a new generation around. You die if you don't buy.

There were earlier pieces of technology that revolutionized libraries. One was the copy machine, maybe the typewriter, the date stamp, and the microform. While I remember an occasional meeting on microforms, it was never attended by library directors, but by technical services people and those responsible for collection development. And those earlier pieces of technology probably revolutionized libraries and collections and the way we manage more than what we're doing today.

But now you find all of the attention going to computers and other kinds of technologies, and you find all the library directors in those programs and the collection development people and the services people are still out there trying to figure out what their role in the profession is. This condition bothers me a lot in that we really need to find some mechanism of bringing the profession together to look at what the role of the library is going to be.

I do wish that in the next 10 years we could connect better with publishers, with authors, with the creators. I'm scared to death of the current publishing scene, the movement away from the old publishing houses, the family publishing houses. No one seems to be paying attention to that. Publishing has moved into the commercial generation of everything from the best seller to the research reports. I hope we don't allow that to happen to our university presses. I'm beginning to see the commercialization move into them. You can see it by the stuff that's getting produced.

When we take something and produce it at the state library through our foundation, there's a real pride, a family pride if you will, in that. What I don't see in the commercial publishing sector anymore is the real familial pride. The old H.W. Wilson Company kind of pride, if you will. You knew when you got a *Reader's Guide* it had been hand-bound by a real person in the basement of that warehouse in the Bronx with a glue stick. There was that kind of pride in it; there isn't that any more.

ASP: State libraries are going to continue to grow in size and in importance. Their planning roles have certainly proven more and more important as change has come faster. A lot of that change has actually been guided and stimulated by planning that the state's agencies have done. That's going to continue and there's going to be even a greater need for it.

Statewide planning for technology has been really crucial and will continue to be, and I think there will be even more of it. Lots and lots of libraries of different types have automated a lot of their operations and we're going to have to link all of those separate automated systems together. It's at the state level where the opportunity to do that will exist, because that's where you can amass the resources. It's where the leadership can come from.

I see it happening already, too, in other areas that really are beyond the library world per se. They may not be the central issues in the library world, maybe they're the central issues to some other groups, but libraries relate to them and have a role in them, and I think it's the responsibility of the state library agency to identify those issues and trends and then begin addressing them, working with the library community.

One that a lot of states have been working on is the role of information and the economic development of the state. Our state [Minnesota] and a lot of other states are going through a real adjustment from a strong agricultural base to having to find new ways of generating growth in the state's economy as agriculture has changed and trying to deal in a whole global environment economically. By identifying an issue like that, we're able to take some leadership in helping guide the library world to realize that information has a major role to play in the economic vitality of a state.

It's information that can help the person trying to start a small business in a rural, remote area that's having to retool to adjust to a new economic scene.

It's information that can help individuals who are going to have to retool themselves to work in a different kind of environment and setting.

Another issue like that is literacy. That has always been important to librarians, but there have been lots and lots of other issues that we see as just as important. It's possible for the state library agency to address literacy from a statewide level and exert some leadership to get local libraries to get involved.

We started in 1983, about the time the Ad Council adopted literacy as one of their national ad campaigns. The literacy specialist for B. Dalton Booksellers, which headquarters in Minneapolis, convened a group of people she thought should be meeting to respond to the national ad campaign. She included the State Library Agency, she included the Department of Education's adult basic and community education staff, the State Literacy Council staff, and other providers of literary services.

From that very modest beginning grew the Governor's Advisory Committee on Adult Literacy that I was privileged to serve on. They developed a long-range plan, and part of that structure was a recommendation for a five-year statewide literacy campaign. The Governor's Advisory Committee turned into a Governor's Task Force, which now has a five-year project for literacy in the libraries, and our agency, too, is very much involved in that. I chaired the statewide coalition for literacy for two years.

The literacy project is going to continue to be a real priority because it does relate again so basically to the economies of the states and the capacity of their people to be competitive and productive workers. It's interesting for librarians because it moves us beyond just getting people up to speed on their reading skills and focuses on their writing skills and computational skills, too. It gives us a different perception of literacy than we had, say 10 years ago, when we thought if we could teach everybody to read, wouldn't that be terrific. Now we're looking at more than just reading skills. We realize they are related to other skills that people have to have, too.

We add new services, so what do we subtract? We don't drop a lot. What happens is that we spend less time on some of the things that we were working more on before, rather than dropping whole services.

We work on an annual work plan basis where we sit down and plan how we're going to invest our time over the next year. Some things never seem to get done and they get carried over on that plan from one year to the next, but they fall on the priority ranking. Other things always emerge.

Our agency, and I think this is fairly typical, has grown a lot in the last few years. I see that continuing. We've got more staff now; we've got a little more money. We've been given more responsibilities by the legislature and the governor because I think there's a growing recognition of a need in state government for an agency that can really address some of those statewide information issues and policies.

SMITH: I'd like to be able to say that we as an institution look at our own service area and look at our demographics and our economic development and the forecast and what the future is or what researchers are saying is going to happen to our community, and that we use that to develop services, and we use that to change or adapt our services.

But I don't think we do that. I think libraries are going to be doing almost the same thing in the next 10 years that we're doing now. We're simply going to use a different delivery method. We'll do it online or we'll use a database instead of pencil and paper. But we won't have changed the service per se. We'll just change the delivery mode. That's because we tend to react, rather than plan and use the kind of information that's available. We don't change what we do, we just change how we do it.

Everybody's talking about the baby boomers and how the '90s will be the decade of children. Well, what does that mean to us? Here we are putting all our emphasis, all our budgets, all our planning and training into technology, and we haven't even thought about technology for children or for families. We don't seem to care enough about what's happening out there. We're simply following the guru of technology, and I think it's going to lead to the disuse of libraries. I'm concerned about that.

The marketing people out there in business, they're noting that there are more kids. They know the impact this technology will have on society, whether it's day care or designer clothes.

Why don't we pay attention to that? Our libraries have the smallest area for kids. Our budgets are the smallest for children. We do the same thing in the public libraries for kids, the same programs that we did 20 years ago, and we can't get librarians to think about how the change in society impacts what we do.

So, if we don't provide something that people want, why should they use us? If our libraries aren't useful, why would you support them? Why would they exist? Unless they're museums, and we're not museums.

MASON: The kinds of services I see developing are extensions of what we have been doing in the past and what we're doing right now. I don't foresee a great revolution in public library service. I see more of an evolutionary process.

The public library is shifting gradually from a place to a service, so that we will be doing more active research, active and interactive research, for the people who use us, often for a fee. I see this coming from the research, the reference background that has always characterized libraries and the new capabilities made possible with the electronic storage and transmission of data.

I believe we will provide better traditional services because of these capabilities. We will become more active in doing the actual research for people, something that libraries have shied away from in the past.

What's the dividing line on fees? Where do you start charging?

MASON: What we charge for is time, the expertise, the professional time of the librarian, a trained researcher.

I do not believe we should be charging for something just because it is machine-accessed. It is not a decision of a patron whether we buy something in book form or machine-readable form (and often there is that choice).

Increasingly in the next 10 or 15 years, I expect more and more material will be available only in electronic format. So if we're going to start charging people only because of that format, we're going to be in trouble, a situation that will undermine the basis for public libraries in this country.

However, I do believe if a librarian spends three hours providing research that will be used by business clients—it could be someone doing research in an academic environment just as easily—at that point, we charge them for the time, just as a lawyer would, or a doctor would, or a consultant would.

I would like to have full cost recovery as opposed to only marginal cost, so we are certainly looking to include an overhead charge. I see libraries running this kind of operation almost like a small business within a not-for-profit setting.

The Cleveland Public Library has recently started such a service. Our charge is $50 an hour. It's mostly for businesses, we've promoted it more to businesses, but it's available to anyone who calls in.

For example, someone was doing research on the use of colors in advertising and wanted to know the impact of different kinds of colors. That didn't take very long, around an hour, I believe. Most of these searches are pretty quick because we do use all the electronic search capabilities available.

We've also done market research for several small companies wanting to locate restaurants in the area. We have done searches for people outside of the area, such as a company in New York that wanted some background information. Apparently they had originated in Cleveland and wanted some historical information that we had easily available, and it's obviously cheaper for them to call and pay us to do the research than it is for them to put someone on a plane to come here to use the library free.

To make the distinction, it just seems to me that the public library needs to continue to provide free access to the range of materials and services we currently offer to people who choose to come in and do their own research. But for people who choose to have us do the research, I think it's quite legitimate for libraries to charge.

Preservation. A lot more talk than action. What's the chief cause for the inaction?

FARBER: Short-sightedness. That is, people's inability to see beyond the horizon. The same reason people are short-sighted about almost anything else. Until it becomes a crisis, one doesn't pay much attention to it.

It has become a crisis and most of us don't realize what a crisis it is because the kinds of materials that most of us deal with are not in a crisis situation.

The things that most of us deal with were published in the last decade or two and we don't have to worry that much about the archival material, or even what was printed around the turn of the century, because we don't deal with it that much. So it really hasn't been brought to our attention. It's beginning to be now.

ROSENTHAL: The effects of deterioration are for a long time invisible, so it's relatively easy to sweep the preservation considerations under the rug. Even if one doesn't consciously do that, or even if one has a strong bent toward acting in the preservation sphere, there are so many other pressing needs.

Actually the Berkeley Library spends well over a million dollars, more like a million and a half, a year on preservation. We get most of it by carving it out of our skins.

We set up a conservation department in 1980 and hired the first department head of conservation. There's been a decided increase in the FTE in the conservation sector, with some of that shifted from the other technical services operations.

Also in various grant proposals that we've made, we have included a preservation component.

DOUGHERTY: I think that we now are taking action.

Preservation has finally reached the top of the priority pile and we're already beginning to see rapid increases in expenditures. It's going to take another five years, though, before we reach the point where the funding level will generate the millions of dollars that's going to be required to solve this problem.

With almost every major issue in our sort of society, the rhetoric greatly precedes the deed. We've known about this problem for years. How come we didn't take action earlier? A problem must reach a very high threshold of pain before it captures the attention of the decision makers. This is a symptom of an overload action agenda.

We've been talking preservation, what, 20 years? And some of the preservationists have known for years what must be done. The trouble was this problem had to compete for our time, attention, and limited resources. All the pieces now are beginning to fit together.

One of the difficult questions we face is in deciding what is not going to be preserved. I was at a conference recently where there was a lot of desk-pounding, primarily by faculty who insisted they had to be involved with the selection of what will or will not be preserved. That process will be painful and it's going to cause a lot of tension and, in some cases, some ill will.

It's going to be difficult for faculty to accept a plan that directs when library A preserves, say, Greek classics, and assigns other areas of the antiquities to other libraries. But such choices will have to be made.

No library is likely to find the resources to preserve all of its own collection. In order to insure comprehensive coverage, libraries will have to work cooperatively. The rest of it is just a matter of resources. If the resources are there, we'll get the job done.

Chapter 2

Library Users in '98

In this chapter, college, public, and school librarians explain how they think users will be different in 1998 and how those differences will cause future library users to have increased expectations of libraries. Most predict major changes.

———— ♦ ♦ ♦ ————

What are library users going to be like in 1998?

McDONALD: One of my visions is that everyone graduating from Foothill College who at least makes the minimum effort of getting to the library is going to know about the information age and is going to graduate information rich rather than information poor. We want students, no matter what they're studying, to know that they can get information that is available to anyone anywhere in the United States. We can get them the same information that someone from Harvard, Berkeley, Stanford, or anywhere else can get.

If students are going to get ahead in the '90s, they are going to have to know how to get information, no matter what field they're in. If they go into the electronics industry, they're going to have to know the most recent research, what is out there in software, and where they can get that information. And they're going to know that they can get it electronically if they've come into our library.

FARBER: People will be expecting materials from anywhere in the world almost instantaneously either in electronic form or in hard form printed or by long-distance facsimile transmission.

That's not much of an exaggeration. There will be a few things that are not available, but almost everything now that's in print will be available to any library, anywhere, assuming it's willing to make the investments in the technology. The user expectation will be more global than it is today.

STEPANIAN: Part of this relates to teachers, and part relates to teacher education. One of the biggest problems is that teacher education has not included library education.

If indeed those new reforms do require some library education in teacher education, then those teachers who are coming out are going to have different kinds of expectations and are going to be using libraries in a way that we librarians think they should be used but haven't been up to this time.

In our district we're taking a different approach to reading, the whole language approach. Some people call it literature-based reading. Basically, it's teaching writing along with reading. The materials that are being used are children's literature. I would like to be able to say that all of our teachers are well-versed in children's literature, but that has not been the case.

All of a sudden teachers are beginning to see the role and the importance of children's literature and all of a sudden it's like, why didn't you tell me these things were here? Of course, they've been there all the time.

We see teachers even wanting to know what's new right now. What's being published in April, they want to have in January. That's their reaction right now.

Our youngsters are becoming very astute at using the micro-computers so we're going to have more and more microcomputer software. We have a lot of it in our libraries right now, but we're going to have more.

Users still want books. I don't think the book is ever going to go away. There are too many people who learn better that way and want to be able to take a book with them and use it in ways we've always used books.

De GENNARO: The users' expectations will be considerably raised. We're already raising their expectations as to what is obtainable from a library through the use of online catalogs, through the use of our new CD-ROM services.

Our users are already getting the idea that libraries are really much more sophisticated and much more capable of delivering services than they have been in the past.

They're going to be making increasing demands on us because we will have whetted their appetites. The question is whether the community and the cities and the people who give us our resources are going to be willing and able to fund the libraries at a level where they can deliver according to these expectations.

DUMONT: It's going to be very important for us to provide information, no matter what format the student needs. We'll have to have in place resource sharing with other institutions. CD-ROM, video disk, and AI will be very prevalent. Everything will be very much interfaced. I see a lot more development in artificial intelligence.

Users will make it very important for the community college to be more than a resource for just faculty and students, to be a resource for people to turn to whether it's in their offices on a PC, dialing into or getting into a major database, or whether it is in an environment such as voice recognition. I see us having to be able to transfer data from one type of system to another.

EASTMAN: Many seem to assume that the library user of the late 1990s won't want to be in the library, that the patron—whether a faculty member, student, or administrator—wants access from his or her desk, that people will find it entirely too troublesome to go to a central source to get information or to get information about information.

I don't think, however, that most intelligent and sensitive people will wish to spend the rest of their lives sitting in one place performing all the functions of their intellectual life.

Furthermore, I truly do not understand, at least in the humanities and liberal arts, how one can have access to ideas without going through the process of what we now call browsing. And that means that you take your body to the material you wish to browse. Just because it's technologically possible to do something is not a reason for it to be done.

The day may come when a publisher will publish 10 copies of a book, produce it in an electronic format, and license people to make it available where they work or live. But still the same intellectual processes have to be accomplished.

I assume publishers will print a few archival copies of every book to assure that it will be permanently available. We know how long paper and binding will last, but we don't know how long many automated products will last or how much use they can withstand. We do know that computerized information can be lost or unavailable when we need it because some portion of the system is down—and may not be up for who knows how long.

When you get right down to it, books are a terribly convenient way to have access to information and ideas. I can start reading a book in my study, finish it in the living room, and in between read it by the swimming pool, on an airplane, in the airport, walking down the street, or sitting on the subway in New York. It can go where I go and I can continue to have access to it. That's not true when you're bound to a particular location by electronics.

MASON: My guess is that the users won't be terribly different. The Booksellers Association has done some studies of people who read, and they tell us that what we're seeing is a shrinking percentage of the population that are heavy readers. But those who are heavy readers read more than they used to.

The literacy issue, I think, becomes a very important one for public libraries as well. It's not clear to me that people who are marginally literate have ever been heavy library users, however.

I expect that the same groups of people who use libraries now will use libraries 10 years from now; however, my guess is that their demands on the library will be more sophisticated. What they want to be able to get from the library will be more challenging for us.

WHITNEY: They're going to be much more adept at using technology. Kids coming into the high schools today already know how to use computers. They have computers at home, they have VCRs at home, they know how to manipulate various kinds of equipment. They can hook speakers up in many configurations. They can take a television and switch the wiring around and do all kinds of things. They're much more adept at using equipment than teachers are. They're not threatened by technology, they are challenged by it.

It is incumbent upon all of us who work with kids in an educational setting to try to improve our own abilities in working with equipment.

Kids also will be much better able to communicate visually than they are today. I am constantly amazed at how students pick up on visual clues. They are much more visual than adults and I see this increasing. It's another area in which we as adults need to improve our skills because they're really far ahead of us.

I hope that kids will be able to think more for themselves, but I really believe the educational system has to change before we are going to see kids who are really able to think critically.

As of now, I don't feel the educational system prepares kids to think critically. I think we tend to put them in classes where teachers lecture to them. Kids are allowed to sit passively. A lot of kids, while they may be in school, are not attentive. They are day-dreaming; they are not really participating in what's going on in the school. Many teachers rely on a single textbook; kids get one point of view, if they bother to read it.

We have to do a lot more with teaching kids to look at a variety of kinds of information and make their own judgments. They are so accustomed now to being told what to think, what to believe, and that's not helping our nation.

Our instruction design capability can do a lot to improve the quality of instruction. We have to get more actively involved, but first, we have to convince others that we do have this ability and have a contribution to make to the instructional process.

SMITH: They're going to be non-White and that has all kinds of cultural implications. Half of society could be illiterate, unemployable.

What we've seen in library user profiles in the past has always been Anglo, educated, and middle class or above. But now we're looking at a society, especially in California, of the year 2000, half the population being illiterate, poorly educated, therefore unskilled and unemployed. There won't be an Anglo majority, there will be a completely ethnic mixture with umpteen different cultural values and languages and backgrounds.

We're not preparing for that. We're not preparing for it in terms of our services or collections or staff. Even when we think of the role of the library, we're asking everybody else to conform to us. We've been successful so we'll stay this way, and all of you have to come to us as we envision you.

I have difficulties with staff now who talk about "demanding" people. I've sort of narrowed that down in my mind that these are people who are generally uneducated, or children, or people who require more than just passive service or passive response. That's a major revolution. Unless we're willing to have blinders on or suffer the consequences of a confrontation, it's going to destroy us.

I'm very concerned about the development of a class society. And libraries are not going to be out there serving the lower classes. They never have. And they don't like to now. So who are they going to serve? It seems like we're going to go right back to serving the original concept of upper middle-class Anglos, and it's going to be a very elitist service again.

Chapter 3

The Effects of Automation

In this chapter, we asked: What impact has technology had on your library? Are there pitfalls? So far, it's online circulation, catalogs, and acquisitions; what's next? Do some users still reject automation? What does serial price inflation do to your collection development? Will the future bring more high-tech people onto library staffs? In 1998, will a massive infusion of electronic databases characterize your library? Do you see libraries and computer centers joining forces? Would that be good? EIDOS, Fred Kilgour's project: Will you join up?

———— ♦ ♦ ♦ ————

Technology—It is promoted as requiring fewer human beings and as a way to lower costs. What impact has it had on your library? Are there pitfalls?

BERGER: It has increased productivity enormously and will continue to do so. But it also has created in some libraries a sweat shop environment of people sitting behind computer terminals all day mindlessly pumping in data. So I don't think it's always been well-handled.

That's a challenge that faces the whole profession throughout the '90s and the early part of the next century to find ways to keep the technology humane while not decreasing the library's productivity. That's not easy.

DOUGHERTY: That's one that the jury is still out on. It would appear with all the technology that's being implemented in libraries, we have not seen any overall reduction in size of staff.

The reductions that are taking place behind the scenes, the technical operations, are resulting in new types of job responsibilities or opportunities. In technical services, we're creating positions like database managers. Whoever heard of a database manager 10 years ago? If we're going to become more involved with activities such as in-depth reference work, we will need more people and better educated professionals.

It's too soon to say whether or not there will be more or fewer staff. My hunch is over time there will be a modest decrease, but I doubt very much, as some technologists currently predict, that a big decrease will occur.

DUMONT: I've been involved in library automation most of my career. I've automated three different systems and have found that, indeed, the costs really aren't reduced.

You might shift them from one type of resource to another, reduce technical positions and services but increase hardware and computer software and technology. The rub on that, though, is that you need a more sophisticated type of librarian to use all the new technology; you need higher-level skills. We thought we'd save money by automating and it would let us provide fewer people to do the job, but in the long run, neither of those expectations came true.

If there are fewer librarians in technical services, those that remain must be highly trained, computer-educated, and motivated to interact with machine-readable databases. Public service librarians will need skills in using computer-based systems and in knowing the types of information stored in various computer systems.

ASP: In the long run it's certainly not going to require fewer staff, and it probably is going to require more. One of my real concerns now is that between 1980 and 1986, the last year for which we've got 12 months of data, the circulation from the public libraries in Minnesota went up 35%. But the staff running those libraries only increased 3%. At some point we're going to reach a breaking point unless that changes.

Automation is one of the reasons the staff didn't have to increase so much, because we've got more efficient ways of doing things. There's been real improvement in planning and management, so that's allowed libraries to stretch their staffs thinner.

The salaries have improved quite a bit. The temptation has been if we can get more salary money rather than hire staff, let's improve the salaries for the people we already have and try and motivate people financially as well as in other ways. But it can't continue, we can't keep having 35% increases in volume of use in libraries and only 3% increases in staff.

The other thing is that a 35% increase in use says that we're really in a high-growth occupation, that the public demand is there, the public interest is there. So the trend is upward and people are expecting more, and they're going to have to have more people serving them when they come in.

FARBER: I don't think it's going to be fewer. It's hard to say if it's going to be much more. Certainly, I don't see any decline in the number of librarians.

What they're going to be doing are somewhat different things. Librarians are going to act much more as interpersonal advisors to individuals on their information needs. As the amount of information and the demand for information both increase, the number of librarians who are going to help people with those information needs is also going to increase.

GORAL: New technologies will allow us to reproduce materials from print to Braille more easily than ever.

ROSENTHAL: Because we've developed an in-house computer system for several major functions of library operations, we have a larger systems office, maybe 13 FTE, than we did. The acquisitions department staffing has dropped and those are the major changes.

There's certainly been a lot of shifting of assignments. Probably 75% or more of the library staff utilize information in an electronic form on an active basis, so that's a marked change.

SMITH: We give it too much emphasis. Its value is only in how it can enable us to be better people. Or as a society, to interface with others in this shrinking world.

Libraries should exist whether or not technology is there. Technology simply makes us do whatever we do a little easier, a little better. But that's not the reason libraries exist.

VASILAKIS: Initially, it's more expensive. It's also difficult to find people who have a foot in both worlds, the "techy" types who can handle the automated world as well as have the service orientation needed in a traditional library setting.

You're going to be looking for people with more technical skills, but still you want people to have that basic service orientation. We have to have those people because they'll be serving library users, the customers of 1998, who have grown up with computer technology from Day One. They'll have had it from grade school on up so they'll expect it.

When I started, you had to have a science background to work in the technical library. Today it's primarily how familiar you are with technology and automation and even things such as AV skills. We're into a lot of different media. People have to be AV experts and PC technicians, and they have to know a lot about telecommunications, how to get things from here to there, but they still need those people skills, too.

WISENER: I do feel there is a negative impact for there are fewer one-to-one dealings. I have well-educated friends who ask me things like, "Is the card catalog going to be computerized?", and they worry about it. It's a real concern and they're smart people. But there's a tremendous generation gap between the computer and non-computer world.

We're going to have to do a large education program. Something unthreatening to train these people. We're going to have to have someone on the job every minute to keep that friendly atmosphere which people do comment on, and libraries should have that above all else, because the user is so important. But right now, it's a very threatening thing for a certain group of people. I'm one of them. I have a hard time, so I know. We may have to do some kind of real campaign for persons who have not run across this elsewhere. That's part of our planning right now. We're going to have to go out there because people don't often come in when they're intimidated. This is a teaching program and no one knows about the new gadgets and if you feel like everyone else is in the same boat, then you'll come.

I visited a beautiful new library recently with a friend, and we were going around and looking at the children's area there, which is all computers, a whole ring of them. This little girl kind of shoved in front of us and she whips through that computer program and she was six or seven years old. And I thought, isn't that wonderful. This is so marvelous. I hope I can do it maybe that well, but I'm still sneaking up on it. I think there are a lot of us.

Another problem, other than intimidation, is that you're not going to be dealing with your users as much. The people stay behind their desks a little more. I always read these articles about how you'll be able to do everything from your home pretty soon. You can order your Christmas presents, you can do this, you can do that, and I think that is the saddest story I've ever heard. It makes me depressed just to think about it.

COOPER: Right now, the older person who loves to read, who reads for recreation and who is sort of the backbone of the smaller libraries and the branch libraries, is really put off by any type of computerization. Now if we don't have literate people or people who are able to use technology, then even if we provide the technology, it won't be used.

There is a tremendous burden on the parent and the school to really prepare people to use a library in their after-school years and use whatever's there. The problem I see is lack of use.

McDONALD: We give people online information, and when they find out how much they really can retrieve on a subject, they are often overwhelmed. Another pitfall is that students often only partially use our systems. They're not trained in information retrieval and they're getting only the tip of the iceberg and still they're feeling satisfied. They don't know what they're missing.

EASTMAN: One is occasionally reminded these days in heavily automated libraries that the new technologies are somehow more "with-it," more sophisticated. It is viewed as more important to be rushing off to worry about hardware and software and hugging sums of money to spend on them than it is to worry about whether the books you ordered six weeks ago have actually arrived, been processed, and put on the shelf.

When you get right down to it, the bulk of library service in most kinds of libraries is still given to people coming in wanting access to books, magazines, journals, newspapers, and other printed data.

And people still want to browse. Not all users know exactly what they want. It is that element of library use that some of the technological systems overlook. You have to know very precisely what you want before you can find out by technological means whether it is there.

But if you just want a good novel for a rainy weekend, you still have to go in and read the shelf. Something will appeal to you—the color of the jacket, the size of the type, the title, the author, whatever—something connects.

But you don't know how to ask on your terminal at home whether the library has Penelope Mortimer's *The Pumpkin Seed* because you don't know without having it brought to your attention that it exists or that it has haunting appeal.

Technology also has widened the gap between the information haves and the have-nots. Automated products—hardware and software—are more expensive than the traditional print sources of information. Money spent in one area isn't there to spend in the other.

The death knell of the book has been rung from time to time across my 30 years in publishing. Yet today more books are being sold and more people are reading more than ever in the history of this nation.

While it is possible, technologically, to provide certain information in a particular way to certain users, not often enough do we hear the people controlling budgets ask whether the number of users, the value of the data, and the speed of delivery are always the highest priorities for the comprehensive library service to a community.

Balance, of course, is the answer. The firm hand of an informed leader who makes major decisions in the context of a vision of what total library service needs to be in the future of the community is one way to achieve that balance. Turf battles between the glitz and glamour high-tech people (who have the capacity to demonstrate the product and "wow" the audience) and librarians who want to use technology appropriately in their situations—in concert with all kinds of media—are heated in some communities. It's difficult to demonstrate the value of a book, or for that matter, of a library. It's what the mind does with all the bits and pieces that matters.

Often because something can be transmitted quickly, the element of speed governs the message, not thoughtfulness, consideration of other options, or efforts to communicate clearly.

Because a computer-generated first draft can look clean and clear, some writers think it has those qualities. Writing is still an instructional activity—one learns what one thinks as one writes—and it still requires a mind guiding an implement—a carving tool, a pen, a typewriter, a PC. But the process of drafting and reading and redrafting and rereading is still the same.

Online circulation. Online catalogs. Online acquisitions. What's next?

MASON: Online reference. I think that's a natural progression. In Cleveland, we have all of that: the online acquisitions and circulation, bibliographic control activities, very well-organized, well-handled at this point.

The next step is the kind of thing that Fred Kilgour talks about with EIDOS. The searching of texts, the searching for text. The biggest problem with all that is developing a profile so that you don't just retrieve everything. There are things you don't want to retrieve.

I frequently tell the story of when I was running the White House Conference on Libraries and Information Services. I had asked a staff member to do a search of all the bills pending before Congress that had anything to do with libraries or information services.

A few days later, the staff member returned with a three-foot stack of paper, plopped it in the middle of my office and said, here it is. What do you want me to do with it?

Well, actually we didn't need all the material. What we needed was about half an inch thick, so there's still that sorting out process. Our biggest problem is becoming not the retrieval but the sorting out.

I remember 20 years ago when I was a young librarian and use of computers in libraries was just beginning, and I said (one of the worst predictions I ever made in my life) that it was never going to work for libraries. I had worked for IBM for a while and I said, the space it takes to contain this information is too great. There's no possibility it can be used for libraries.

Now, of course, it's laughable when we can put 250,000 pages on one CD-ROM. It certainly is possible that we can do a great many things that we never thought we could do before, and it's even beginning to look like libraries may be one of the more appropriate places to use some of these new capabilities.

Do you still have a portion of the faculty who say, pox on this electronic stuff?

ROSENTHAL: There will probably be a few hold-outs, but I see the process of change among faculty members as occurring quite rapidly.

A surprising number of faculty members in the humanities disciplines, for example, are willing, eager, and in many cases, able to use information in electronic form. Already to a very considerable extent, information in an electronic form is used widely by scholars in the social sciences.

As a critical mass of scholars becomes used to dealing with information in electronic form, it will be seen as a necessary skill.

Inflation and the cost of serials. What does this do to your collection development?

ROSENTHAL: Well, it makes things very difficult. We were fairly successful for the years 1975 through 1985, in keeping the serials allocation about 50% of the overall library materials budget. And Berkeley has a tremendous serials collection, one of the biggest in the country.

In the past two years, the percentage of the total library materials budget that's taken up with serial subscriptions is now over 60%. What it means is that we've had to curtail the purchase of monographs and cancel about $100,000 worth of serial subscriptions.

For the future, there will be the burgeoning opportunity to acquire information in electronic form. This is an add-on cost. We cannot curtail acquisition of publications in book and booklike form simply because the electronic stuff is available and yet we must to some degree or other cope with information in electronic form.

I see very tough times because the economic situation is going to make it very difficult for academia in general and for academic libraries in particular. I also see a 60–70% possibility that the state will become less and less willing to increase on a straight line projection allocations for library materials.

Whatever happens, we cannot reduce our book allocation enough to match the cost of information in electronic form. It's an add-on, not a substitution. That means in the library at Berkeley, and I suspect in most of the research libraries in the country, we are not acquiring to any degree of comprehensiveness significant publications that we should be acquiring. Significant publications in English as well as in foreign languages. Significant trade book publications, significant university press publications.

DUMONT: Community colleges are very current literature oriented, so we try very hard to keep a good base of periodicals and serials. The higher prices certainly are having a devastating effect on our budgets. I don't know where they will stop.

Certainly, electronic publishing will provide some relief in the future. If we can't get enough relief that way, we will probably begin resource sharing with specialty serials. We'll have to.

A university that has a large research program in nuclear physics will probably end up being the major resource center for that type of literature, for instance. And community colleges may end up being the major resource for a particular type of education they provide, perhaps technological training or agriculture or high tech, whatever their emphasis is.

Probably what we'll have to do is find some way, some fee-base, to reimburse the libraries that have the resources being used. I don't think there is any way we can continue to say that free access should be the rule. Those that have the resources that are willing to share them ought to get reimbursed for their use.

That's going to happen more and more into the remainder of this century.

In the future, do you see a lot of high-tech people, not librarian types, coming into the field?

VASILAKIS: We've always looked for people with sort of a technical bent or some sort of scientific background because we felt they could relate better to the scientists and engineers who use our library.

But what's happened is that as our products matured, we have become more business oriented. We've gone from supporting scientific researchers to supporting the internal business organization and assisting in market research. We look now for people who have all these skills and know how to use the business databases and the databases that relate to statistical information, census bureau data, and competitor kinds of information, strategic planning kinds of information.

So we're looking for people with a general business kind of background we can train to be aware of Westinghouse's interest.

We want them to stay ahead and make sure they know what our strategic planners are interested in, so they can be proactive. And let's face it, we are also looking for people who understand the need to market the library itself. If you add value and no one knows it, where are you? The librarian has to think of the library itself as a mini-business. We want people who are intelligent, who can be trained, and who will identify with the mission of the organization. That's a key, too, that they believe in what they're doing; it's an okay thing, and they have an interest in it. Having that interest in your company, knowing your company is all-important. I guess I'm talking about company loyalty.

What will change is our method of document delivery. It's got to get better. We still need to retrieve information faster, and that focuses again on the centralized databases.

I see there is a danger in database services pricing themselves out of business if they're not careful. A lot of libraries are looking at being more selective; people are looking for quality. We'll get to the point where there's so much out there, we'll start looking at what are the best quality databases and use fewer better ones.

CHISHOLM: With computer applications and the newly developing technology, we're seeing a really tremendous increase in the numbers of persons coming from math, science, and computer backgrounds. We're getting a much larger number of persons who come with backgrounds in another subject area and then plan their career. If a student wants to become a science librarian, he or she will take a master's degree in science and then come to librarianship.

Also, I see persons getting a Ph.D. in another subject area, particularly if they are interested in a specific discipline. If they want to go into archival management, they'll get a Ph.D. in some aspect of history and then enter the graduate program in librarianship.

I see that careful planning, getting another graduate degree prior to coming into librarianship, is becoming more common. This is also a time for persons with backgrounds in computer science. Some high-tech people will enter the field, particularly in database development and database management, and in research and development for new high-tech products.

SUMMERS: I see that in a Toynbeean kind of sense. We went through a period of that in the early introduction of computers in the libraries where some of the early information scientists went around saying librarians can't do this because they don't have the perspective.

We worked through that and the field sort of drew in that technical perspective, and it became an expectation that librarians not only could, but would.

We've gone through it again in the sense that we need people who look outside of the traditional institution, and you've seen a number of library school dean appointments, major ones, going to folks who are not librarians and who have a presumably "techy" kind of orientation.

I think we'll move through that again, because the values and issues that are crucial are social, political ones, not technical. And nobody's got a monopoly on the right kind of social and political attitudes and values.

WEDGEWORTH: We're going to continue to see a mix of backgrounds in those who are employed by libraries and those who direct libraries. But there's no question that the professionally educated librarian and information specialist will continue to dominate our field.

Individuals of talent will always find an inroad no matter what field that you're talking about, but I don't see any indication that we will lose the dominance that we enjoy in our field. When people raise that question to me I point to the success of American librarianship and I say, you go with the people who got you where you are.

Certainly, individuals can come in to deal with a particular problem, but the most enduring support that libraries and organized information services have had and will continue to have will be from those who are professionally educated to guide and direct their operation.

HEIM: We've been under the impression that we've had to have those kind of people because of the automation development. But we're in a second stage of automation now. Many libraries are already automated.

So that while everybody will be more of a computer expert, and the library of the future will look more technological, I don't think it's going to be different people doing technology. It's going to be us, people like me with a degree in English who just wanted to do these things.

We'll look more high-tech, but we'll be the same in terms of our commitment to information access.

Ten years from now, is your library going to have a massive infusion of electronic databases?

BERGER: Electronic databases have reduced our collection, particularly in law and in medicine. For example, we have projects in the area of biotechnology. For over 80 years we have had an arrangement with the American Dental Association to develop and test new dental materials. (I might add that the high-speed drill was invented here, so if you've not suffered in your dentist's chair recently you can thank the Bureau of Standards for that.) Sometimes we don't resort to hard copy at all to answer the kinds of questions that come out of such programs. We go online to find the answer.

In chemistry, there are structural databases which enable the searcher to identify a molecule or a radical—a cluster of molecules—by simply drawing the structure on the screen and then searching the database of structures for similar molecules, compounds, radicals, or whatever. That kind of thing cannot be duplicated efficiently on paper.

Prior to the advent of databases, the best the staff of this library could do was to teach the scientist how to use the bibliographic tools. There was no way in the world that they could undertake research for the scientist, because there were too few staff members to manipulate time-consuming paper bibliographic tools and data compilations. Automation has changed all that. We now have some 265 online SDI searches we update at least once a month.

WHITNEY: Yes. CD-ROM is moving into schools at a rapid rate. More and more schools are going online with databases. The way to fund that is a problem, and most schools are violently opposed to charging kids for those kinds of services, so until we find some way to fund this without passing the cost onto the kids, online databases will continue to be a problem.

But CD-ROM holds real promise, particularly for school libraries. Online catalogs are here now, and I see more and more of us moving in that direction. Hopefully, within the next three to four years we will have online patron access. Circulation systems are probably 50% of high school libraries, maybe approximately that in elementary schools. Microcomputers are moving into school libraries. We spend probably $3,000 a year on microcomputer software.

Collections are definitely changing. And collections are no longer solely housed on campus. We have to be able to reach out and tap resources all over the state, all over the nation, in order to really serve the needs of our students and our staff.

For example, journals. I can never provide all the journals that we need. And we turn to the interlibrary loan center for help. I've gotten journals from France that have been requested by teachers, and we have to become more comfortable using outside resources because our kids and our faculty need access to those resources.

SMITH: Sure. Why not? If we had a massive infusion of books, we'd add them. I don't see that they're any different; they're just another delivery mechanism.

DUMONT: I don't know that everything will be in electronic database form. Perhaps in CD-ROM or video disk form, certainly in machine-readable form. I don't know if it's going to be a massive infusion. The book is still going to be here, but for current information types of resources, we will have other sources of machine-readable databases.

FARBER: There won't have to be a massive infusion of electronic databases because almost any database can be accessible over a simple telephone or whatever replaces the telephone, so that the information will be available on a combination screen, voice and picture equipment. People will be able to dial up the information as they need it.

One difference will be that there will be a lot of things in the new kinds of microstorages, some form of video disk or whatever replaces video disks in 10 years. There will be a lot of things on-site and libraries will be able to pack much more information on this new kind of technology.

Libraries and computer centers: Converging? Is that desirable?

DUMONT: The first system we put in at Dallas Community College, which was the first Dataphase system in the country, worked on a minicomputer that was in my area. I was solely responsible for the upkeep, maintenance, and running of that minicomputer, as well as trying to put on the software and making sure that all the bugs of a very new system were working out.

I did that for five years and I can assure you that it was a happy day when the computer center agreed to take over the hardware and its maintenance. For me it was a very frustrating experience to have to provide the hardware and the people to maintain the hardware, while all I was interested in was concentrating on development and implementation of the software and service to the users.

There is a danger that we as librarians must be aware of, and that is we must not allow the computing people to try to be all things to all people. They see that as a very strong power base. We as librarians have had the training in management of data, and we must continue to perfect that and prove ourselves worthy of being the managers of the data and the databases. I see that either continuing, or we will end up being only clerical people.

MASON: You have libraries and you have computer centers and there is some overlap and there are some distinctions.

There are some things that computer centers do that have nothing to do with libraries, maintaining personnel records, for instance. There are other things that libraries do that have nothing to do with computer centers, such as maintaining books. But there are significant areas where there is overlap and I don't see that changing functionally for a good long while, even though there may be some forced mergers.

McDONALD: Not for us. We work together closely, we each have a donated Tandem computer, and we try to make sure that data processing remembers that we have our mainframe computers that need to connect and interface with the student information system and the management information system.

FARBER: At our institution we put the computer center into the library some years ago. That was done for two purposes.

One was to make it a part of the entire campus, because the library is regarded as part of the entire campus; it is not belonging to any one particular department. And the computer center, which had been in the science area, was felt to be becoming too much a possession of the scientists, and the president, rightfully so, wanted it to be looked upon as an institutional resource rather than just a resource for the scientists.

The second reason was, and this was what made me so happy, that it made the library a total information resource. Our audio-visual services also are in the library, so that whatever form the information was in—print, microform, imagery, or now electronic—the library would be the one place to go for it. For fund raising or development purposes, this made a lot of sense.

But I'm in charge only of the library. The computer center is under someone else, and the audio-visual services are under another person. The three of us work together. For example, we're planning an addition to the library and the three of us have been meeting with the architects and talking together about the plans.

ROSENTHAL: There's been a fair amount of interaction. There has not been convergence. But in general, the climate is good. I don't see a convergence in terms of organizational structure for a while.

DOUGHERTY: There are lots of opportunities for cooperation because a convergence of activity interests is occurring. But some have argued that libraries and computers would be combined. That is unlikely. Computing folk now realize they are more at risk than are libraries because of distribution of mainframe computing.

Computing officials are now asked to be accountable. Tens of millions of dollars have been spent on campuses to develop technological info-structures. But where are the benefits? Where is the improvement in the quality of education of students? There's very little evidence to date that we've done much more than create the most powerful word processing system in the world.

Traditional mainframe computing operations are being broken up. And the campus computing czars built their empires on computing environments. We should applaud the efforts of our colleagues from computing centers; they have helped to create an enormously powerful set of tools. It's our forte to use those tools to do what we've always done, that is to work with information.

EASTMAN: If large numbers of people and large numbers of dollars are merged into the library from a non-library source, the computer experts could take over. We might see the same pattern we saw in school libraries, 10, 15, 20 years ago when some of the remarkable people—mostly women—who were state, city, and county school library supervisors retired. Their successors were audio-visual people, usually men, who were not librarians and did not understand libraries. School library service was not strengthened as a result of that evolution.

The same pattern I think could be repeated in academic libraries if computing and library services were joined under the leadership of someone not a librarian or not wholly sympathetic to the library point of view.

EIDOS—Fred Kilgour's project for retrieval of information from within books in electronic form. Will you get into that?

HEIM: I'm sure EIDOS would spread rapidly if it really was up and running and easy to use. We now see students who wait in line to use the computer terminal even if the card catalog is still there. Students are very accepting of new technology, especially at the undergraduate level.

SMITH: Sure, why not? The Kilgour program on full text information will be very helpful because people want the text, they don't want just the citation. That's what people are interested in. Besides, it's direct. It's not like going from one train station to another. You just go to the source. I think people will want that and it will be extremely useful.

STRONG: If I can see something enhancing the service capability of the people that I've got working—the professionals on the line day in and day out who have got to deliver answers in a public policy context, usually in a very short time—I'm going to grab anything I can get. This looks like it has that kind of potential.

I don't know at what costs, though, or what I have to give up in the process of getting to something like this. I also don't know what society will give up as users of information if we undercut the institution of the library too much.

Part of what bothers me in a proposal like this, if I really understand it, is that it bypasses the existing organization of information to the point where we may not even have the collections then, they will all be somewhere else.

I still am one of those hard-line idiots that believes that one of the last institutions left in our society that treats the individual as an individual is the library. If we lose the collections and we lose the organization of those collections and the logical organized access to them for the broadest of the society, we've lost the last institution in our society that really respects the individual.

Machines don't respect the individual. And systems that allow the elite of our society to have preferential access over those who need interpretation—Help! I think we really need to do more assessment of what the real societal impacts of EIDOS are.

ASP: I've heard publishers say for years that since they're already using computer-generated databases in their operations—for typesetting, for copies, for authors—that something ought to be done with that because the format exists. So I think Fred Kilgour's ideas are definitely going to happen.

I think what there will be, though, is many providers of that kind of full-text service. It's not going to be just OCLC or one entity. Some of the publishers are so major that it's going to be to their financial interest to themselves offer that service to which libraries would subscribe. In fact, I think there are a few that are already moving very, very fast in that direction by offering full-text access to the same computer-generated files that they're using to produce print books; you can buy it in print or you can search it online. I think librarians are going to have to deal with multiple entities in that, but it is going to improve service and speed up access to information.

It's not going to be the whole answer because there are certain things you don't get in that kind of a system. You can't cuddle up with your computer terminal or your printout in bed—it's just not the same feel as having a book. If you're accessing information and you're trying to scan something on a screen, it's not the same as scanning it on paper.

You lose a certain amount of serendipity. I would think researchers could probably remember times when they were wandering around the stack in a library looking for maybe a particular item, and it turned out the item next to it was the one they really wanted. There's some of that that's lost when you automate all of this, so I don't think those systems are going to replace a lot of the print sources and the services. They're going to be added to it, and they're going to be a way of insuring that we can get instant access to things that now we can't access, as Fred Kilgour points out, if somebody's checked it out or if it's lost on the shelf.

Twenty years ago when I started working in libraries I used to think, wouldn't it be wonderful if we could wire our shelves so that they could buzz when we tried to put a book in the wrong place, because so much information was lost if somebody misshelved something. It is the same kind of notion that we're so dependent on catalogs now and we're so dependent on things to be in order to meet people's needs.

But now that there are newer generations of computer equipment on the horizon, and the capacity to do full-text storage and full-text search, that is going to be a major breakthrough for an add-on to library service and a speeding up of information access.

FARBER: Well, something like that. It's imaginative, but I don't think it's far-fetched at all. I think that's going to come.

GORAL: Mr. Kilgour is someone who has vision, who looks to the future, but I see EIDOS as both a positive and a negative thing.

It will allow people to do their own general reference work. The reference librarian will then have to be much more specialized, much more technical. But you still will have the person who comes into the library who really needs a good reference interview, and you're not going to be able to get that on a micro. People walking in who really don't exactly know what they're looking for, but they can kind of give you a general idea what it is they want.

EIDOS will either pick up the general reference questions that don't necessarily need to be picked up by the reference librarian or else the general reference interview will take place and then it will be much more specialized going into EIDOS, so it could go either way.

If we could get the funding, I'd like to see our library becoming an active partner in EIDOS.

ROSENTHAL: I have some reservations about the particular construct that Fred sets forth with relation to OCLC, but I do think that in general the library will be offering a panoply of information along those lines.

The extent to which a library goes in that direction is going to be somewhat discretionary. Do you emphasize advanced research and scholarship in terms of training and information and the provision for services, or do you emphasize advice on how to write a term paper to undergraduate students?

There will be a whole range of programs and there will be limited amounts of money as to what you can do and limited amounts of staff time. So you've got to make some choices.

There's a tremendous range of information becoming available and we would certainly not want to depend on any one organization for a complete range.

McDONALD: I don't think EIDOS will become standard procedure in our community college library. It sounds in some ways more suitable for a public library.

It was interesting that the plan that was proposed excluded fiction, which makes sense. Most people don't want to curl up with a computer at night. But it also excluded reference information, which I would have thought was what the system was best at delivering.

For information, EIDOS is certainly feasible, but there's the other part of librarianship, which is knowledge, and there is a difference between the two. I think EIDOS will be adequate for information, but there are a lot of systems delivering this now and EIDOS is only one of many.

Chapter 4

What Works Best in Getting Your Budget Approved

No library can be at its best without a reasonable budget, and in this chapter, 15 of our leaders share dozens of the best ways they have found to get their budgets both approved and improved. Keeping everybody well informed is a general theme, but also see the comment about what university presidents will fund just "because that's what's fun."

———— ♦ ♦ ♦ ————

What's your best argument for getting your budget approved?

ASP: We've done reasonably well compared to other states. What I've tried to do is cultivate as many lobbyists as I possibly can. Make sure that everybody is as informed as possible about what the department's position is on the budget. Try and encourage supporters of libraries, Friends of Libraries, to contact legislators, and then the legislators to contact the governor in support of those budget requests.

It's been when we have a lot of that kind of involvement from the library community as a whole that we have had success. Telling the story—as people have known for years—telling the story of your needs in human interest terms is still really important, and snowing legislators with statistics and data isn't going to have the effect that giving them three or four stories of folks who have benefited from the service will.

I had an experience in the legislative session in '87 that was one of those delightful ones I hope will happen again. The chair of the Senate Education Finance Committee, after listening to the budget presentation, gave a testimonial for how wonderful interlibrary loan was and how he himself had gotten materials from Harvard and the University of Illinois and other libraries. And he said, you folks in the libraries really have that structure worked out when you can get for me, in my little house in Wyoming, Minnesota, all of these materials from all over the country. He told the story far better than I could and was in a position to do something about our budget.

We also should pay close attention to the services that we can provide the government. Government people need quality information and we're the specialists at providing that.

Over the next 10 years, we need to do more of that. I've seen in bigger cities that city libraries have accepted responsibilities for serving their governments. I haven't seen it happening as much in medium size and small cities, and I'm not sure how much of that occurs in colleges and university libraries, but I think all of us can benefit more if we realize that our libraries to a great extent are special libraries, specialized collections for the people whom we depend on.

A city should look at its public library as its library for its own operation. The management of a college or university should look at the campus library as not just supporting the research of the faculty and students but also supporting the operation of the institution and being able to get information they need to make management decisions.

De GENNARO: Selling the money-providers on the value of the library.

Vartan Gregorian is a master at that. When Gregorian talks about libraries, it is inspiring. He's reselling the New York Public Library, reselling libraries to a broad constituency of supporters, and he does it by reaffirming old-fashioned values which some of us find difficult to express. We hesitate to talk about patriotism and learning because it's a rhetoric that has been misused by a lot of insincere people, and we're reluctant to talk in those terms.

Gregorian has been particularly effective because he doesn't have those inhibitions. He has come into our culture from the Middle East, and he's able to speak plainly and simply. I think a large part of his success has been his willingness, his ability to talk in ordinary, familiar terms about the importance of knowledge, of learning, and of libraries as the repositories of the records of civilization.

Another thing that he has to his advantage is that he's not a librarian and therefore can appear not to have a vested interest in promoting libraries. If I talk about the importance of libraries, the audience is apt to say, "Well, yes, Dick is a librarian and spent his life at that and has a vested interest in pushing libraries, so what else could we expect him to say?" But when it's said by a Gregorian, or a Billington, or a Boorstin, these kinds of things get a better audience than when we say them. Of course, these people seem to say them more eloquently than we do and that helps enormously.

So back to the question, how do we get the money? We get the support by convincing our supporters of the importance of the institution and that has to be done on general, conceptual terms.

I think the same thing could be true of the new technology. I talk about new technology and where things are going in the 1990s and you could ask, "Where are you going to get the money to do that?" We're going to get the money to do that, if we get it at all, by talking in broad, conceptual terms about how this is going to be important to the people we're trying to serve.

That's why I stress how we're going to bring information services, in whatever form, to the poor people in the neighborhoods, to the middle-class people, to people in their homes, how we're going to bring the contents of the library out of the library and into people's lives.

You've got to have big ideas to sell to big people. That's the way they think, and if you can convince them that you have a vision of the future, that you have the competence to make it happen, people will want to buy into something that's going to win.

If we keep telling them we're poor, that we're starving, that we're failing, and that we're losing, and it's only with their help that we're going to succeed, we'll fail for nobody wants to buy into a dying institution. So we have to convince our supporters that we have a future, that we're vital.

WISENER: A very good budget with a lot of explanation and understanding of where our goals are. The librarian keeps city government folks informed weekly, monthly, all the time, what's going on, where we're having troubles.

GORAL: That we are the only resource available for any particular clients in the state of Colorado. We're not dispersed throughout the state, we are one agency. We service all of the residents of

Colorado who are eligible for LBPH services. That pretty much keeps the hounds at bay. They cut, but they don't necessarily take as much as they do from other agencies because they know that ours is a service our clients cannot get anywhere else.

DUMONT: Being able to communicate to the people you report to the needs that you have, that you are indeed providing a service that is needed. Again, it is that very important interaction with what the faculty and students need to teach and learn. You are a partner hand-in-hand with the faculty. You mustn't neglect to let your superiors know about this.

You have to always keep in mind that you are working with students who have a need, perceived or unperceived, particularly in a community college. It's very gratifying to see a person grow in knowledge and become better than he or she was when he or she came to you and who now wants to go on with a love of learning. Education is providing them with the skills they need to make a living, to have a job, to provide for their families, and to contribute to their community. These are all things you have to keep clearly focused when you ask for budgets. What is it going to do to help others? How are you going to help others in your learning resource center, in your library?

We are there to provide the support needed for the faculty to do their job. Not many community college people do research and only a few publish a great deal. They're not necessarily requirements in our institutions.

But good teaching is. Good teaching skills are. That's our strength. Continuing to provide the services to support teaching and learning is our only real way to ask for budgets.

McDONALD: Our administration has been supportive and they have a way of saying, you bring the service in, you bring the program in, show us that it works for a year or so, then we'll fund it.

It comes out of our hide, usually, the first time around. I offer new services first, you know, put the carrot out there and the money follows.

I didn't ask for money for online information retrieval; I just introduced it and fiddled with my budget. After we did online searches for the president, the chancellor, and a few faculty, then, of course, no one could live without it.

BERGER: The staff in this place. If they don't have what they need down here they raise hell with their own managers.

The government, as you know, has a terrible time competing with private industry for top-flight scientists because of pay restrictions. And several of them had said and written that the two things which attracted them to the Bureau of Standards were the outstanding research library and the research facilities in the laboratories.

Like other scientific libraries, we are having a tough time because of the Reagan Administration's policy to let the dollar float. As a result, journal prices have just simply gone out of sight. The Bureau is doing its very best to cope with that. They are making available to me all the resources that they can. However, it's not enough and we have had to cut our journals. In addition, we were ordered by the Administration to take staff cuts in the early '80s. Those cuts have never been restored.

As a result, we can no longer give full service at the circulation desk. We're open only from 10 to 4 there. The same is true of interlibrary loan and the same is true of the reference desk. I hate it, but I'd rather give top-flight service part of the time than lousy service all of the time. Those were our options.

I never lock this library. It's open seven days a week, 24 hours a day to anyone affiliated with the Bureau of Standards. We have over 900 research associates and foreign guest workers, as well as our regular staff of 1,700.

Library staff serves them only from 8:30 to 5, but my loss rate is no greater than that of other libraries. Of course, our titles are perhaps not the most thrilling in the world. A book about Newton's Third Law of Thermodynamics is not apt to be a best seller!

The scientists are very good about checking out stuff after hours. They're very good about signing in also because they understand that if I can't demonstrate that this place is used, it will be closed. We've had several attempts to make us close after hours to "save money on electricity," that kind of nonsense. One of the ways you deflect those kinds of arguments is by being able to show that at 2 a.m. on Christmas Eve, there was indeed somebody in here monitoring an experiment and in the library working.

There's nothing routine or even standard about science. If an experiment requires you to work at night, that is what you do, and that's when you need access to the library, not during the day.

We're trying to develop a set of protocols which will enable the user to go online with DIALOG and some of the other databases when we're not here and at least get answers to simple questions. In part we've accomplished this already, because five years ago we began training laboratory staff to do simple searches.

I can't expand my staff, but I can give the scientists a password to DIALOG, train them to do easy searching, and reserve our work for those projects requiring searches of four or five databases or unfamiliar databases.

FARBER: It's just doing a good job. I have a very cooperative administration, an administration that appreciates what I do and I think understands that I don't ask for things that I don't need. That I don't exaggerate my budget because I know that the institution is going to cut it by 10%. In this case it's a different kind of situation because it's a Quaker institution, and people take you at your word. So there's no finagling, no bargaining.

WHITNEY: Students and staff have to have access to resources if they are going to learn. And that's the most effective argument.

When you look at our periodical list and start trying to determine where you can cut and not really hurt the kids, you can't do it. I mean if you cut one title you severely restrict their access and so we've been very successful in maintaining our budget.

Ten years from now our most successful argument to get budget is going to be the fact that as our students go off to institutions of higher education, they have to be familiar and comfortable using a variety of sources. They are going to encounter CD-ROM at college. They're going to encounter patron public access catalogs. They're going to need to know how to search online. They need to be familiar with basic reference tools. They need to have read widely. All of those are arguments that are hard to refuse.

And the students who are not going into further academic work but are going down the vocational trail have even more needs, probably, than the kids who are going on to college, because we must prepare them to be lifelong learners. We must establish an attitude in them that makes them comfortable with using public libraries, finding information in a variety of sources.

The kids who are starting school this year will graduate in the year 2000, and it is amazing to think that we are preparing kids now for the twenty-first century. Change is going to be the most challenging force that they will have to face, and the only way they can successfully adapt to change is to be able to continue to learn. They have to be able to adapt as society changes.

They can't do that if they are not comfortable with finding information, if they don't know how to define what they need to know. Information is the key to success in the future and that's our challenge—the key to success, and also the key to survival.

ROSENTHAL: Most of the budget for the Berkeley library is formula-driven and is pretty well decided by the formulas and by the state budget.

I and my colleagues in the other libraries of the University of California have only a minor role to play, an indirect role, in trying to augment budgets. What we do is, over the course of several years, try to make a case for augmentation programmatically.

Sometimes we're successful, sometimes we're not. Sometimes there are negative happenings, such as in the past two years the University of California libraries got in one year no budgetary increase at all for library materials and in the second year, an increase of only about 3%, which has been very bad news as far as library materials go.

We have been successful to a certain extent within the University in getting money for capital projects after a hiatus of close to a decade in which very few library buildings were built or renovated. That looks as though it's on the upswing.

And we've been to a very modest degree successful in instituting a state allocation for preservation of library materials. It's far from sufficient—a total of $200,000 a year for all nine UC libraries.

CHISHOLM: Keeping an administrator totally and completely informed. That is the most effective way to present a strong case, to present the rationale, to be sure the person, budget committee, or administrator in charge understands your program and understands your rationale and your goals.

DOUGHERTY: My arguments also reflect my style.

For example, I could not get foundation funding for our residency program. We needed about $600,000 and when I asked the Provost for support I promised to cost share and to take over the program's full funding after three years—and we did it. We're now in our fifth year.

All vice-presidents are constantly besieged for resources by every dean on the campus, and the choices a vice-president must make are rarely easy. The vice-presidents I've worked with usually place higher priority on requests when you're willing to use your own money. I've funded a number of projects on the basis of cost sharing.

The most persuasive argument, at least in the universities I've been associated with, is based on peer relationships. It's the strongest argument I've been able to muster up. In California, for example, the legislature didn't give a whit about what Harvard or what Yale was doing, but university officials did. And so we always look very closely at what our peers are doing. If we happen to be doing well vis-à-vis our peers, our arguments for more dollars are not likely to fall upon responsive ears. So long as you maintain your competitive position with whoever are your peer groups, the reasoning goes, users of the library will not be disadvantaged. But if the library begins to fall away from its peers, or if the perception begins to trickle out into the field that the institution is falling behind, that could have implications for the institution's ability to compete.

I have never consciously tried to arouse the faculty against the administration, but sometimes that can happen, particularly when the book budget is involved. In such instances the library director can get caught in the middle between the faculty and administration. In such instances I must represent the faculty; that's my job. If I don't I will certainly lose faculty support. On the other hand, I'm part of the university administration. So far I've been lucky; I've only been accused of blackmail once and the vice-president did it with a smile on his face, and he gave me the money, by the way.

My strongest argument is to be honest. I do my damnedest to; that's the way I was taught by my mentor in library school, Ralph Shaw, who said tell the truth, don't deliberately try to pad your budget. Go in and ask for what you need and then fight for it. If you don't get it, that's the way it goes. Sometimes you're successful, sometimes you're not.

I've tried to use innovation to justify budget requests. Sometimes you get vice-presidents who like that and who are willing to go along with it. I recall once Harold Shapiro, until recently president of the University of Michigan, suggesting to me that presidents will sometimes fund dreams and visions because that's what's fun. I've tried not to forget that point.

Grant money helps. It gives you credibility that oftentimes will result in local support.

But your major argument, really, in my experience, is the peer relationships.

STRONG: After Proposition 13, the number of Friends groups in the state doubled. It's taken citizens saying no, you won't cut my libraries. It's taken boards of trustees that have become—instead of nursemaids to book sales and out-of-date collections—advocates for library services at the local government level. We have over 200,000 Friends of Libraries that we can call on in California to talk to their local legislators, to their city council people.

So one major way to be sure you're going to have enough budget is by building political awareness. And it's also the reality that we've brought people to the point of realizing that their libraries could close, and they didn't want them to. And as we do so well in the state, people speak out.

It was the leadership on the one hand of good management, or at least adequate management, plus the building of the political awareness. Building of a legislative core.

Our champion for state aid to libraries was a Republican, a conservative Republican from the northern part of the state, Jim Nielson, who carried that public library funding bill three, four, five times before it got passed. I mean, conservative Republicans aren't supposed to give you more money. What that coalition put together was an incredible movement to say libraries are important. And all we did was capitalize on that.

SMITH: Now it's my reputation. I enjoy the confidence of the board of supervisors, all of them, and my staff. The community already is supportive of libraries, so it's not that difficult. Orange County puts a value on standards and process of packaging and documentation and such. My success in the past assures it in the future.

I earned that reputation by being convincing in promoting the role of libraries. And I just assumed I would be successful. The studies on self-fulfilling prophecy have something to say to us and as a profession we need to listen. If we aren't our best advocates, I don't know who else is going to do it for us.

I have a healthy budget. But, if I didn't, that wouldn't mean I couldn't do what I wanted. It simply would mean that I would select what I wanted to do with whatever resources I have.

People talk about priorities and compromising or not doing this and doing that. We do that with our personal lives. We sacrifice something to get something else. That's no different from the way you run a library. Everyone has a budget. It's what you do with it and how.

I'm really tired of people talking about money. Money is not always the answer. It helps, but it's not always the answer. It's as if librarians are waiting to get more money so they can do something. They'll never do it, because they aren't going to get more money.

VASILAKIS: How much value does it add to the organization? How does it help us sell products to the customer, and what value does that have?

We're continually selling. Once a month I write a report which goes to my management. I will select those items that helped us sell something, helped us make the product better, improved the quality of our product. These are the things that we're measured on.

When something works especially well, it is recognized and our people are nominated for quality awards. I think that Tom Peters, in the *In Search for Excellence* book, really had an impact on corporate America. It has really filtered into the way we do business in our libraries.

In our corporation, we're out there competing today globally. We feel we've got to survive, we feel we've got to add value, we've got to pull our weight, pay our way, and believe in what we're doing.

Chapter 5

Library Schools

Everybody, it seems, knows what library schools should teach, and this chapter includes comments from both deans and directors and also from non-educators. They consider how the library school curriculum should change, the leading challenge for the schools, the biggest changes they've faced recently, how the cost of the new technology affects their programs, and whether the field attracts the best and the brightest students.

♦ ♦ ♦

The library school curriculum: By 1998, how should it change?

DOUGHERTY: I see the need for a greater relationship between practitioners and the educators. Oftentimes we sort of say, well, what we have to do is become oriented in a more interdisciplinary manner. There's no doubt law, journalism, communication, computer science, management, all impinge on or are contiguous to us in an intellectual sense. But from a logistical sense, just try and develop linkages with these various schools. It is very difficult to do.

For example, when the school of management wants to develop an interdisciplinary thrust, do they come over to the school of journalism and negotiate? No, they appoint someone on the management faculty to take care of it. They've got the resources.

Our library schools are too small; we don't have enough flexibility. We must find ways to expand the number of faculty so that we can begin to address some of these interdisciplinary concerns.

When I went to school, we had cataloging laboratories which were used to help students illustrate cataloging principles. Learning principles was considered more important than learning the "how-tos" because faculty realized when students took a job in some library the chances were very high that the library would have its own interpretation of the rules, its own policies and procedures. Whatever you learned about the "hows," you had to throw out and learn how they did it on your new job.

The same with database searching. The student will gain from exposure in a laboratory by getting some hands-on experience with database searching, but the how-to-search-a-database is not what's important. It's understanding the concepts on which the database is structured and organized.

We're spending a lot of money in our library keeping our most skilled people up to date because most databases are in a constant state of change. So what they learned in library school is, in many cases, outdated before they get into their first position.

It's like when you go to medical school; you're going to have to learn the bones and there's memorization involved. But too many library schools have focused to the extreme on the "hows."

I also think that too many of the faculty are out-of-date. They don't know what's going on and that's unfortunate.

I've heard practitioners complain that if only faculty would "take their sabbatical and go work on a reference desk, they would become better informed about what's happening." That's nonsense, and it isn't going to happen; in a way it's demeaning. Nonetheless, the problem of updating faculty is a real one.

Faculty do keep up with the literature. They're not keeping up with what is going on in the libraries. There's not enough interchange between practitioners and faculty.

There are steps we could take to improve matters. We have to create incentives so that faculty will want to reach out. One frequent complaint is that practitioners make faculty who attempt to reach out feel unwelcome, or worse, inferior. We've got to work harder to build a partnership.

The problems we're experiencing aren't very different from those that exist between medical school clinicians and educators.

WISENER: The library schools need a more dynamic program.

I found this in my education program too. My first major was psychology and it was exciting and it was fun and I switched to education and every book said the same thing. But there was nothing exciting and it wasn't even challenging.

I feel that library schools suffer the same way. I think they're sort of blind. I think all they see is the new technology.

I know from our experience and from talking to librarians that they're closing their children's service training areas. Now that makes absolutely no sense to me, for when we needed a children's librarian, we've had to go to education areas, we've had to go into other degrees entirely.

They ought to get those children's programs spiced up too and get some innovative ideas. Get some enthusiastic people. You need to show that there's life and excitement in your future if you become a librarian. Make your program as exciting as it really is.

Include real entrepreneur programs. Include all the political advocacy that you can possibly teach and the importance of that to good leadership.

Students should study speech, almost all the same things that lawyers have to have. They should learn to speak, be able to think on their feet. They need to have a Toastmasters course within the school.

One more thing that should be included in library school and isn't, as far as I know, is working with trustees, working with Friends, using them properly. Learning what advocacy is from a citizen's point of view.

CHISHOLM: Even today, our beginning student must be able to understand a computer and do online searching within the first week in the library school. However, not all students pursue a comprehensive curriculum in which they deal with a great variety of applications of technology. In the future this will be changed and the application of technology will be a required part of the curriculum. There will be no options, it will be mandatory. Utilizing technology will be a skill every library student will be expected to have.

We will be attracting a somewhat different kind of student into librarianship. There will be a much greater likelihood of attracting persons with science, math, or computer science backgrounds. Much of the curriculum will move rapidly into the more sophisticated computer applications and utilization of databases through online searching.

Courses in management and administration will become required courses. Public speaking, including oral presentations to governing groups, I think will also be mandatory. The level of sophistication will escalate quite rapidly and dramatically into much more demanding courses on management and administration, database development, and computer application.

McDONALD: Library schools ought to be emphasizing indexing, because automation is based on understanding the bibliographic record. Library directors in the past came from heads of reference, but today, I also see some of them coming from heads of technical services. Technical service librarians really do understand how to automate the library because they understand the bibliographic record, which of course is the basis for library automation.

FARBER: Obviously, the curriculum must introduce students to more of the technology, to reflect the changing library.

Whether or not cataloging will still be taught, I honestly don't know.

Whether reference will be taught, should be taught, or taught but not in the same way, I don't know.

Two things I do think will happen:

One is the study of information science, how information is transmitted.

Second is how people learn, the new developments in cognition. That will be much more important. I've seen a difference in the ways students learn, in the ways students interact with the new kinds of information technology, and I'm thinking particularly of CD-ROM.

Up to now, we have had to accept the databases and the indexes, the structure of those databases, and use the terms that indexers gave us. Now that's all up for grabs.

Using the new kinds of CD-ROMs, let's say, a student can manipulate a database and can use his or her own terminology and so learns in a very different way, and so reorganizes the database to meet his or her own perceptions and needs. That's a whole new way of learning and interacting with the information itself. I think that librarians are going to have to study much more of the cognitive sciences to understand how people learn, how they interact with the information itself.

HEIM: Students will come in knowing basic microcomputer use so we'll be able to start at a higher level of technology, a higher level of automation skills.

I hope that as we become more interdisciplinary that we will draw from a broader range of students in the sciences and social sciences than we have in the past. And then these students themselves will drive curricular changes as they develop librarianship along the lines of their thinking, not in our traditional mode, which has been humanities.

Currently we have taken humanities-oriented students and transformed them into technological wizards. That's one way to do it, but I think we'll have more people coming to the field who have these other backgrounds already.

I'd like to see us be the center of the university and have double master's degrees or joint master's degrees with all other disciplines on campus. We've worked to have a computer science double master's; we're working on a public affairs double master's. And art history. We are continually getting a flow of art history majors wanting to get a library science degree or literature majors wanting to be reader advisors or collection development people in academic libraries.

I dream that library schools will move from positions of marginality on campuses to positions of centrality. Everybody who goes to college needs to understand that the skills of a library information professional are skills that they should have. Ideally, everybody would have a library science degree or at least a component of it.

Information literacy is important to survival today.

COOPER: I do wish our library schools could give more time to helping students learn the skills of dealing with the public and with organized citizen advocates. They need to learn how to deal with trustees and learn that they should mobilize people as part of their job.

SUMMERS: The contents of the various sub-specialties in the field are going to be very much more proscribed and probably expanded.

Right now a library school can claim a specialization in some subject and support it with three or four courses—or even only one special elective in addition to a group of other rather basic kinds of classes.

I think the field is going to say we need specialized people and we're going to insist that they have a special kind of preparation and that will be true in school media services, medical librarianship, a variety of other sub-specializations. Those are going to become very much more clearly defined and very much more rigid and probably very much expanded.

WEDGEWORTH: What we see coming in the next decade is upon us now.

We have seen out in the field, since the beginning of the 1960s, what I describe as a quiet revolution. It hasn't attracted a great deal of public attention.

You do get local public attention when a particular library automates or brings in a bank of computers or hooks up to some special service, but much of the technical work methods that we were trained to use when I came out of graduate school as a librarian at the beginning of the 1960s, either we don't do it anymore or it's done entirely differently from the way it was done.

Specifically, I talk about the techniques in describing and classifying books by subject. We used to do that by hand. Now most of that material is done via computers.

We used to receive printed cards from the Library of Congress or from the H.W. Wilson Company, or one of the other service companies, and we would modify those cards to go in a local catalog.

There are a few libraries that continue to receive cards directly from the Library of Congress, but most of the libraries that continue to use card catalogs either produce the cards locally or get them from some other service. Even if they're using the catalogs, most of them are involved with some kind of network where they share bibliographic information, the descriptions and subject classification of books and journals and other materials.

That was the beginning of the revolution, the back-room kinds of activities. It has now spread to users; where users used to consult printed indexes to journals, they now can go to online databases. They now can go to other kinds of computer-readable data like the U.S. Census tapes available at some large research libraries. There are many different formats and materials, the most recent of which has been the optical disk to store materials.

The changes that I'm referring to are principally driven by technology, but the cost of that technology is so expensive that it has forced new demands on library management.

As we look into the 1990s, we see we'll have to prepare librarians to be much better managers.

They've got to have much stronger financial management skills, they've got to have much more demanding analytical skills to be able to analyze operations and set them up to operate efficiently and effectively.

They also have to relate to many different kinds of users.

In public libraries, for example, the libraries have gone back to focusing on literacy. We have to see what illiteracy means in the late twentieth century and how to effectively combat that.

We've called attention to the literacy problem, but we haven't developed very many new programs for addressing it at the local level with the understanding that it's not likely that we're going to have any massive federal assistance to help this time around, as we did back in the '20s and '30s when we were still dealing with large immigrant populations mostly from Europe, rather than from the Far East as we are getting now.

Changes that I see in the curriculum will be more financial management courses, more statistical and analytical courses, stronger courses in user education to teach people how to use libraries, stronger understanding of users from a sociological point of view.

We're going to be much more involved in teaching people how to understand many different types of technologies.

We'll also be crossing over to many other graduate departments, more so than we have in the past, because the schools in our field tend to have fairly small faculties and that means you can't offer advanced courses in certain areas to the extent that you would like.

But why should you when you have on your own campus a business school, you have a law school, you have a department of sociology, you have a department of English or history, all of which offer relevant courses to the graduate study for librarians?

EASTMAN: One thing they could do is to teach more people to be better managers, to prepare them better to be administrators.

Perhaps in the future people who are going to direct libraries of a certain size, and handle budgets of a certain size, should also be required to have a master's in business or some substantial business experience. Library schools will have to strengthen their curricula in this area.

People who are going to run libraries have to learn the business side of it somewhere. They're not learning it now in most library schools, and this is a real problem because some library directors are responsible for huge sums of money and large staffs.

What's the #1 challenge for library schools during the next decade?

HEIM: Recruitment of bright students.

If you start with good, bright, inquiring, intelligent people, the schools will get better. It all flows from those that we recruit. While there may be challenges in terms of not getting enough equipment money, or fighting with university budgets, or worrying that the management information system of the business department is going to take us over, the real challenge is to continue to recruit bright and intelligent and risk-taking students.

They will solve it all for us, or help us to solve it.

SUMMERS: To build credibility on campus for the program by expanding the research productivity of the library science program.

Library education suffers badly in its image with colleagues on the campus because we don't have the same kind of research activities that other disciplines do. If we want our image to change, that's got to change.

Library school programs are generally better regarded than schools of education simply because people think what we do is important and also, we do it better and with less of the traditional kinds of criticism.

We're not as well-respected as schools of engineering, schools of medicine, schools of business, because they couple sound educational programs with sound research and public service programs. We haven't yet done that.

Some of us do a fair amount of public service, but it's not public service in the sense that other disciplines do it. Most of us don't do very much in the way of funded research, which is a growing expectation in other fields.

We get judged on the same yardstick as all the rest of the disciplines, as we should if we want to be in universities.

If we don't want to be in universities, then we don't have to be charged with that and we can go back like we used to be—training programs connected with libraries.

But if you want to be in universities, the expectations are sound teaching, funded research, and public service of a high order, not routine. We have to live up to that measuring stick and that's the major challenge.

WEDGEWORTH: The same as the challenge for the libraries. We've got to build quality.

Currently there are lots of discussions about another librarian shortage as we had in the 1960s.

In the late 1960s we said we had a shortage of 100,000 librarians. We opened a number of new graduate library education programs to fill this need, we met that need, and now we've seen a number of schools—not necessarily the weakest—close.

The real pressure has come on the private universities that offer graduate library education. Many of those programs were the strongest in the region. But the competition within private universities for resources makes it tough on small departments and as a result, the graduate library education programs, along with some other small programs, have come under severe pressure and we've lost a number of those departments.

This time around I don't think we ought to respond to the shortage the same way. I think we ought to take advantage of the opportunity to build stronger educational programs for librarians, create jobs that are more responsible, that require a broader and stronger education, and in the field we're going to be looking at the same kinds of improvements in quality.

We've got to deliver services more effectively from larger collections. We've got to deliver materials that are more precisely relevant to the questions that researchers and students ask us for.

So the challenge is basically the same: improve quality.

Since you began in administration, what's been the biggest change in library schools?

SUMMERS: Education of librarians moved from being a relatively low unit cost to a relatively high unit cost discipline.

This happened in part because of the increase in the cost of technology. It costs more now to run a library school. Fifteen years ago to have a pretty good library school, you needed a small group of faculty and a pretty good library. You could run, like they do in English and history, large sections of classes and the unit costs were relatively low.

Now we have to have a lot of specialized classes, a lot of specialized faculty, a lot of specialized equipment, and that means the unit cost goes higher.

Obviously, those unit costs would be lower if enrollment were higher. But even with that, they'd still be higher than they once were, and I think we're moving from being a discipline that one might think of like English, where the incremental cost per student is relatively low, to one more like engineering, medicine, or law, where the incremental cost per student is very high.

By 1998, the unit cost may peak out and maybe even decline because I think enrollment is getting ready to go back up. I believe that society has a dramatically increasing need for the kinds of things that we prepare people to do.

Has the cost of the new technology been inhibiting the adaptation of library school curricula across the country?

SUMMERS: I think so. I think it's had a very significant impact on the fact that we see library schools closing up. Institutions are simply saying we're not able to or we're not willing to pay that kind of cost. That's one impact it's had, very definitely. But also, schools have not been able to adopt technology at a uniform rate and, once they get the hardware part, have not been able to utilize it in terms of software and access to other kinds of databases. That has inhibited the rate at which they could convert their technology.

For example, most library schools today have a course in which they teach students how to search online databases. There's general agreement that that really ought to be taught on a subject basis. That is, when students study information in the humanities, they deal with the online humanities databases. When they're in science and technology, they deal with those. It's obviously more expensive to teach it that way, and so virtually all library schools are driven to compress all of that into one online course, despite the fact they'd really prefer to distribute it throughout their curriculum. That's a perfect example of a case where cost is impinging upon curriculum.

How much has it cost you to keep your library school up to date with technology?

CHISHOLM: Some of the basic equipment has been purchased by the state, but if I would have had to depend on the normal university budget, I never could have purchased the equipment to furnish the lab. Now we have a very well-equipped, well-stocked, large computer laboratory due to the support of many loyal alums and others. All the equipment cost a total of about $300,000.

SUMMERS: At South Carolina, $50,000, $60,000, probably $70,000. At Florida State last year we spent about $80,000 on technology, and this year we're probably going to spend $50,000 or $60,000.

At both institutions, I was able to fully equip labs for students and give all faculty members a PC on their desks and that type of thing.

1998. How much are you going to have to spend between now and then on the technology?

SUMMERS: That obviously depends upon the rate of technological change.

I would expect that the dimensions of the technological change are relatively apparent. That is, we know that people are going to be handling information on personal work stations that they control.

We know that we're going to be looking at denser and denser mediums of storage and that the costs of storage are probably not going to decline significantly, because they've already declined an enormous amount.

We know that people are going to be looking for alternatives to online kinds of systems because they don't want to pay the communications cost.

Beyond that, I think we're going to see a much tighter wedding between television and computers and the whole notion of interaction. That's probably going to be the major technological impact that will have cost implications.

I couldn't put a dollar cost on that but I think those are some of the parameters of the problem. I expect that it will be as dramatic as the kinds of investments that have been required to bring a school to a ready state of technology today. The incremental costs are going to be there, but not at the same magnitude.

CHISHOLM: To stay up-to-date for the next 10 years, I estimate will cost another $750,000 for new equipment and software.

Should all M.L.S. programs be two years?

CHISHOLM: I have to answer that with great ambivalence.

If you're talking about an ideal situation and an optimum curriculum, then yes, it would be very nice to have two years. There are so many changes, so many new developments, and so much currently that students must learn, two years could easily be filled with classes which would not be redundant.

But the other side of that coin is that we now have extremely high tuition. It's very expensive for students to attend graduate programs. Very few scholarships will pay the full way. Relatively few research assistantships or teaching assistantships are available.

The disconcerting part is that librarianship is a very low-paid profession, and so to expect students to attend graduate school for two full years, to go into debt, and then go into a very low-paying position is expecting real sacrifice.

If we are going to consider only curriculum, we could very well do an excellent job with a two-year curriculum and give students excellent preparation. At the same time, my concern for students keeps me from saying we'll do that because I think it's a disservice to the students. It would require that they spend all that time, money, and earning power, and then go to a job that's not financially rewarding.

SUMMERS: We've never done an adequate job in defining what is really essential and whether we are delivering that in the most efficient kind of way. Until we do that, you can't really answer that question.

It may be expanded; it could even be contracted.

We have this notion of a basic core that everybody has to take, and in most library schools it's occupying an increasingly large proportion of the total. If one were to look really critically at that core, perhaps it could be reduced or in many cases eliminated. If one were to do that, then the need for expansion might be very different.

What's the quality of students in library schools?

WEDGEWORTH: That will vary from one school to the next. Here at Columbia, we can say that the top two-thirds of our students would hold their own with the students in the other parts of the university.

I get students into Columbia who scored the highest scores on the Graduate Record Examination and I get students into our school who are right on the borderline for the Graduate Record Examination across the university.

Still, you also have a substantial number of people who are coming back to school some years after they've completed their undergraduate education. They're a little more difficult to assess. Sometimes they don't perform as well on the Graduate Record Examination, which is our most general indicator of quality across the university. Then again, sometimes they even pick up a few points, if they haven't been out of school too long and they've been involved in some kind of academic-type pursuit.

I have had the question asked, "Are the students as good now as they were when we came along earlier?"

Our students are as good or better than they have been in the past. In fact, the average student coming into our program knows more than the average student who might have come in before 1960. They've been exposed to more. They have broader ranging academic preparation. On the other hand, they don't cluster culturally as tightly as they did before, so the variation in knowledge and experience in a given class is much greater today than perhaps it was in, say, 1959.

As a result, it's more difficult for the classroom instructor because you've got to be sure everybody is on at least some kind of common level before you can push them into more advanced material.

How much do the people in the field affect your curriculum?

SUMMERS: No library school can get very far away from the expectations and beliefs and attitudes of the field it serves. If one tries to depart too far—and at the University of South Carolina I was involved in an innovation that was attempting to do that—inevitably you're going to get some degree of discreditedness and some degree of forcing you back toward the main.

The field chants a lot about innovation but it is like most fields, I guess. It wants innovation in kind rather than degree.

So I guess we listen a lot, but you have to recognize that we also have the capacity to influence what the field says because many library educators are very much involved in the profession. As a result, we have an impact on what the field says to us.

It's not incidental that I'm president-elect of the American Library Association. The person currently president is a dean; there have been a series of deans of library schools in that position and in other leadership positions so that library educators are not simply at the whim of the field, but they influence the message the field gives to that audience.

Why doesn't library work and why don't library schools attract more of the best and the brightest?

WISENER: Maybe library schools need a little poke in the arm. They're a little uninspiring. You get all excited about the field. You get admitted to a library school and then what happens there dampens your enthusiasm. They don't offer as much as you expect. But once you leave, once young librarians get out in the field, it is exciting. It's a joy.

But maybe prospective students don't even choose the school because there's a certain dullness that they sense.

SUMMERS: In part it's our ability to articulate the nature of the work. We don't always think what is really satisfying about this kind of work, what's really stimulating about it.

I've been in this field I guess 40 years, I started when I was 14. I've not had a day that has not been stimulating, in which I have not learned something really new, and I don't think there are many professions about which one can say that.

I don't think we do a good job in demonstrating that. We don't have a good system of peerage, in the sense that folks in libraries take a heavy responsibility for looking out for the brightest and the best. Some do, many don't. There are people who see that as part of their professional role, to seek out young people, but there aren't enough of them.

I think we're the kind of profession that most folks don't come to without some positive exposure. We still have all too many situations that reinforce the old, negative kind of image.

We need to find better ways to identify and communicate the excitement about the profession and we need to find ways, better and quicker ways, to get rid of those situations that reinforce the stereotype.

EASTMAN: Salaries in the library fields are a national embarrassment. You really have to want to be a librarian for a whole lot of reasons having nothing to do with income. The field is 80% to 85% female. Any field that is so heavily populated with women is overworked and underpaid. That's the way it is in this country. Look at nursing, elementary education, publishing. And look at how few top jobs in librarianship are held by women. More women direct public libraries than college and university libraries, despite the fact that this is one area in which academic institutions could hire women for top jobs and thus improve their EEO/AA statistics. And there are plenty of capable women out there.

HEIM: We're sort of a hidden profession. Ninety out of 100 think the person at the check-out desk is a librarian. We have no visibility. Asking campus freshmen what field they want, 0% say library science. We do have a low national image, a low national visibility, and ALA is working very hard to correct that.

If I can talk to anyone for 10 minutes, I can convince them that librarianship is the most important job in the world.

COOPER: I don't think it's the nature of the work, I think it is the pay and the image.

Librarians should project the image of young to middle-age professionals who have exciting jobs with contact with the public and who are doing work of first class. But right now not enough of them do this, and librarianship doesn't rank with some of the other desirable professions for many people.

But when I see the type of work librarians do, especially in the public library field, it's so exciting and so complicated. In my system, people have the opportunity to move laterally and move all around as opportunities open up. They never sit on the same job for 25 years. They are constantly learning, gaining new skills, meeting new people and challenges.

I see at ALA so many people whose work is just as exciting, and who are as qualified and as competitive and as able to express themselves, just on a par with any career.

GORAL: Ah, but library schools do attract some of them. And I don't think the nature of library work turns off people who are bright, who are intelligent. I think sometimes it attracts them.

It's a profession where you have information and you have the power of knowing what to do with it. Just the power of having the information and knowing what to do with it makes you a very powerful person at times. That's coming across, the power of the information age. We will be very, very important in the future. We really need to look at ourselves as being powerful people.

CHISHOLM: I think the field has attracted its share of the brightest. As proof, if you look at the Graduate Record Exam scores of entering students compared with any other professional school or any other graduate program, we in librarianship compare very favorably. In some years, we're at the very top. We attract very bright people, but they tend not to be the visionary, convincing leaders that I believe we need. They have the potential, but they haven't been encouraged to take on that kind of responsibility in the past. They must be encouraged to do that in the future.

WEDGEWORTH: I just don't see the evidence of that. I think that one of the specific characteristics of the library field is that we tend to be harder on ourselves than anybody else is.

If I look at the Phi Beta Kappas that I know in the library field, they don't wear their Phi Beta Kappa key or pin, but we have our complement of people who were top academics.

We have our complement of people who went to very strong colleges and universities for undergraduate training; we also have a preponderance of our people in the field who have humanities backgrounds. Therefore, their quantitative skills and knowledge probably are not as strong as you would find in other fields. That's not to say that our people are lacking in quality or they're lacking intelligence.

It simply hasn't been demonstrated to me—no matter where you pull the students from, whether you're taking from a small school in the South, or the Midwest, or one of the stronger schools with a large population—I just haven't seen any evidence that librarians are less well-prepared than in the past.

What is a general phenomenon right now is that all of the graduate and professional schools are suffering because of the strength of the med schools and the law schools and the business schools.

There's been a real dramatic shift to the top performers into those three departments, so that the graduate library schools and the other professional schools that don't present as lucrative careers as those three have tended to suffer.

Chapter 6

New Qualifications for Entry-Level Librarians

To be really ready for the next century, new entry-level librarians will need to be better at communication skills, analytical skills, human relations, understanding cultural differences, and more.

———— ♦ ♦ ♦ ————

Ten years from now, what do you see as the new entry-level qualifications for librarians?

SUMMERS: I see four areas that are the most important:

One, we'll need people who have a much better grasp of fundamental, effective communication abilities, both written and oral. I'm not talking about them taking the kind of courses we traditionally teach on how to communicate in groups. We need to produce people who really have the ability to be quite articulate presenters of ideas and people who are good at synthesizing thoughts and writing and speaking, making a case, that kind of thing.

Two, there will be a demand for people with much greater analytical ability than we have had to date. I mean analytical both in the sense of numerate, that is the ability to analyze problems from a statistical point of view, and analytical from a logical point of view, to look at a question and discern what are the root issues and how one labels and identifies those and deals with them.

Three, we're going to need people who have the ability to do technical synthesis, and that is to look at a lot of technological alternatives and pull out a synthetic solution that is efficient and effective. I don't think they're going to need to be technicians, but they need to be able to make an effective analysis of technological situations and reach a good synthesis.

And four, we will still have to have people, and this has been a persistent need, who have attitudes and values that are consistent with the viewpoint that how and whether people in this society get information is an important question. That has always been fundamental in the field and will continue to be even more so.

The whole notion of what society needs and how it will get its information and who will ensure equitable distribution is a very major public policy issue that's going to be resolved in the next 10 years. We have to produce people who can be articulate and persuasive and who can help resolve this.

HEIM: They will need to be more schooled in organizational politics, whether they're going to universities or higher education administration or public libraries.

We talk a lot about the political process, but the nation is becoming increasingly political in all aspects and the good entry-level librarian, probably more than anything else, needs the organizational sense, a political sense.

VASILAKIS: The library schools have to train tomorrow's professionals to be both high-tech and people oriented. These people will have to know their way around PCs and know how to handle electronics. It will be a hard job.

They'll have to know the sources of information; that's not going to change. No matter what happens, all this technology isn't going to do you any good unless you know what is where and where to get it. That will stay the same—absolutely.

Primarily, people will have to know how to program or at least be computer literate in addition to knowing the basic library things: sources of information, how to organize, how to get information to people.

ASP: A major thing that we are going to get back to is more of a recognition of the importance of the human interrelationships, the user/staff member interface. The last 10 years we've been so immersed in looking at technology and how to use technology to control our information, to access our information, to make our operations more efficient that we've turned libraries to a great extent into kind of self-service supermarkets.

The staff members you encounter when you go into a library as a user often times are not professional staff; they're support staff, they're clerical staff, and the professionals are in the back managing the operation and doing the behind-the-scenes kind of work. That didn't used to be the case.

I'm hoping that we will be able to move back to relating what's in the library and what we can access through the technology to the individual user. Then when people come in they will realize that there's some person who's got fairly extensive, detailed knowledge and training and experience in communicating with individuals, and translating the individual's request and information needs into the structures and systems the librarians know about in order to retrieve that information.

I'm not sure that the library schools are going in that direction, but I think that will be a real important qualification for somebody getting into library service in the future.

We're already experiencing a shortage of children's librarians fairly widely in the country. There's a shortage of people going into school library media work in our state and in other states, too.

Maybe some of the humanities-type folks we used to get into the field have gotten turned off by all the emphasis on technology and have found careers in teaching or social work or some of the other service professions, thinking that all librarians are doing is playing around with machines, and they wanted to work with people.

Maybe we can start getting back some of those folks who want to work one-on-one with people and get more involved again in the kind of outreach work that librarians need to do so desperately.

GORAL: Probably having more expertise in database searching. Having more information about libraries for the blind and handicapped in general.

I don't know of any particular library school that has a specific program for a student interested in libraries for the blind and handicapped.

They need to be aware of the technology, the databases, the microcomputers, voice synthesizers and the other equipment that will be available to the blind and handicapped. It's difficult to come into the program cold.

STEPANIAN: They are going to have to have a better background in electronics and in video. It's the same thing that happened when AV became part of the library—people became so involved in AV that they didn't know how to organize materials; they had no idea what kinds of services the library offered.

What may happen is that it may take more than one year to earn a library degree even though I'm not sure that we can afford it with what we pay librarians. I just think there's so much more to learn. And I don't think that you can take away any of what's taught now.

BERGER: There will be a fairly good supply of librarians with a strong background in science. That has not been true during my career. With two exceptions on my staff, every M.L.S. I've hired I've had to send back to school to take at least introductory courses in chemistry, physics, mathematics, and statistics. It has been so very difficult to find librarians with even a working vocabulary of the hard sciences. That is changing.

WHITNEY: Hopefully, by 1998 we will have defined more clearly the educational preparation necessary for the entry-level school librarian.

As it is now, people come into the profession from a variety of educational backgrounds, and our new national standards for the first time state that a master's degree is the entry-level degree, but do not define all the course work that is needed for that master's degree.

There's still not a consensus as to what are absolute essentials for school librarian preparation. I see that as we move into the twenty-first century, the instructional design component is going to be more widely accepted as a basic requirement. Some of us have it now, but a lot of us don't. A lot of school librarians come in very poorly equipped to deal with computers. The technology training is not yet there, but I think that will certainly be accepted as essential by 1998.

And more and more we're going to realize that we need people who are bilingual. That's going to be more of a requirement than it is now.

ROSENTHAL: They'll all have to be familiar with bibliographic systems in electronic form because online catalogs will be the primary catalog access for our staff and for our users. That's happening very fast.

In addition, most reference librarians will need to be familiar with database access and will need to be knowledgeable about non-bibliographic databases in the sphere of their own expertise.

Aside from that, I don't know that the qualifications will change a great deal.

In all of our positions where there's contact with the public, we emphasize the ability to communicate in oral as well as written form with the clientele. And that depends not only on one's intelligence, but on one's skills in the reference dialogue and in ascertaining what exactly the query is.

That will be very important because in many cases the contact will not be face-to-face. And communication is far superior when you have face-to-face contact. When you're dealing on a telephone or computer terminal to computer terminal, the librarian will need particularly sharp skills in order to be able to find out precisely what the queries are.

MASON: I don't expect a large change in what we require. I would like to see some changes in the people we get with those requirements, and that goes back to how we attract different people into library school and what they're taught when they get there.

My guess is that we will expect an entry-level librarian to have a master's in library science as we do now. One of the reasons for that, especially in a public library environment, is that our needs are so broad.

We need, on the one hand, children's services librarians; we need catalogers; we still do use catalogers in a library like Cleveland, even though we buy most of our cataloging; we need specialists in, say, city planning.

In addition, I'd like to see more aggressive people. More entrepreneurial types.

When we were hiring for the individual to run our research center, which is the fee-based service, it was very difficult to find someone first who wanted to do it, because it's very much an entrepreneurial activity, and who also had the personality characteristics to find that exciting. I don't think everyone needs to be like that, but we do need a few more.

McDONALD: The same as for the staff I've just hired in the last two years. They have to be able to search online. They have to be visionary and understand that we are always going to stay right at the forefront of automation, and that they need to understand not only automation but also service, giving the very best service we can in the most efficient way.

Librarians today need to be manager-type people. Many of the jobs that librarians used to do are now being done by automation and by library technicians. Librarians need to be service-oriented and also management-oriented.

I would look for staff who would use automation in new and creative ways. We have automated our manual systems, and we've transferred the old standards over to our new automated systems. Now let's see what automation can really do for us. Even the systems we have now can do a lot more for us than we're asking of them.

More and more libraries are going to be hiring library technicians with automation skills. Ours are encouraged to take on more responsibilities. I'm always amazed when someone says, why would a library technician need to know anything about the new AACR2 cataloging rules? Well, they're doing most of the copy cataloging online, and they need to be able to upgrade records and understand what might be wrong with the online record.

WEDGEWORTH: We're going to have to look to a stronger differentiation of library employees. At the same time we're creating more responsible jobs for librarians, we've got to create more responsible paraprofessional career opportunities. That's very clear.

You see many older, large libraries that still take in large numbers of beginning professionals. But they can't offer the kinds of exciting opportunities that a small corporate office can offer them to come in and organize an information service.

Therefore, some of the best graduates coming out of this program and others are going into special information work.

It's quite common to say that it's the money that attracts them. Certainly, the young people are interested in money, but what I find out from talking with them is that they're perhaps more interested in being able to do something significant from the very beginning.

They don't want to go in and serve an apprenticeship for five years before they get to supervise three people.

So we're going to have to have complete restructuring of library employment, especially in our larger institutions. In some of our smaller institutions we're going to have to adjust to the fact that we may not have a librarian in every single branch, but we may have supervising librarians engaging in very strong training programs so that we don't need to be concerned about the public calling someone a librarian.

We'll have library clerks and library assistants and other categories of employees who can carry out a broad range of functions that are sometimes assigned to professionals now in small institutions.

But I think that communities and institutions will find that they can't afford to employ graduate librarians to do those kinds of jobs. So we'll be forced to look differently at how we deploy and train staff in the future.

DUMONT: We all will have to be computer literate. We'll all have to have a knowledge of how computers act, how they work, how they interact with our lives personally as well as professionally.

Librarians will continue to need the analytical skills that a liberal arts education can give us, to be able to reason and think and deduce what people really want and how to find it. We're certainly going to have to have a knowledge of where things are and how we can get to them. Perhaps each one of us is not going to have to have absolutely all of this massive knowledge of every single thing because the amount of data, after all, is doubling every few years.

But it still will be an enormous amount of data that our survival as a profession will depend on. And it's probably going to be more difficult for any one of us to know where everything is. Having to be able to interact with people and provide service to them via all this information means librarians are above all going to have to be people-oriented. Librarians will become more specialized, but we must learn to use all the other technologies that can help us do our job easier and provide the service that we say we should be giving.

We're living is a very exciting phase of our profession right now. We are in the midst of really moving out on this edge. Of course, it can be a very bad time to be a librarian if you're really not willing to change, but it's going to happen and I think we need to prepare ourselves through our training, our knowledge, and our intellectual abilities to really stretch out and be imaginative.

SMITH: They're going to need new languages and skills and training in cultural differences. And the same kinds of training that businesses now put their staff through when they go to work in another country, which is what California is going to turn out to be; it's going to be a "foreign" country.

We're also going to need people who are service-oriented, who like people, and who have a sense of commitment to the profession and not to the job. You're not going to get wealthy in this profession, and I don't know that this generation or the next generation is concerned with anything other than their own standard of living. So where are we going to find people who have a sense of social responsibility and see a value in libraries through working with people?

We've always said we're for everybody, all ages, everybody. But we've never really been that. Now in California we're going to be forced either to eat that or face the fact that that's not what we're there for.

STRONG: I was on a program on that subject recently, and one of the speakers said he couldn't find a whole lot of individuals who possess new basic competencies that are needed. We need to update our understanding of the world in which those competencies have to function.

The professional entry-level librarian ought to be a manager, ought to be a leader, because in most libraries these days, with so few of us left, any entry-level librarian might be a branch manager, might be in charge of that library reference desk nights and weekends, and he or she had better be a good manager or we'll end up giving lousy service.

A couple of things that I look for in a professional, entry or otherwise:

One is compassion, an understanding of the people who are to be served. I don't think we've talked very much or thought very much about that in the profession as a part of training. Understanding the role of the library in the society we live in today, or maybe better said, an understanding of the society, so that we can position the library better.

Let me give you an example: We do a civil service exam, and I serve on the oral interview panel for the principal librarian examination at the state level. That's for our top department heads, consultants, major consulting positions. I am continually appalled at the number of people, seasoned in the profession—you have to be to even take the exam—who, when I ask them, "Where do you see libraries five, ten years down the road?" can't tell me. They have no vision of what we're supposed to be doing as an institution, as a profession, of anything. I think people ought to come in with a little bit of vision, at least.

And then last I'd add passion. I think we ought to love the profession we're in. We ought to be committed to it or get out. You gotta love medicine to treat people. You gotta love the law to be a good lawyer. I think you've gotta love librarianship to be a good librarian. And I don't think you need to apologize to anyone for that.

FARBER: I don't see them much different from today, frankly. I still think that a good solid undergraduate education, a good well-rounded education, and eclectic interests are terribly important.

The second thing that will still be very important is an interest in higher education, the purposes and methods of higher education. The other things will be taken care of, it seems to me, by the changing curriculum in library schools.

Chapter 7

Continuing Education

This subject never was more important to professional librarians. Has it kept up or is it falling behind? Should it be mandatory for the continued certification of all librarians?

———— ◆ ◆ ◆ ————

Continuing education: Has it fallen behind?

CHISHOLM: There are many problems.

If practicing professionals are going to be kept up-to-date, they have to know about the utilization and application of technology. Some librarians are reluctant to do that. They have a psychological barrier. They don't want to deal with technology. They're being forced to deal with it and they don't like it.

Another problem is providing the equipment, the software and the computer laboratories. Availability is costly.

There is some difficulty in getting persons knowledgeable and capable enough to serve as instructors and then to transport them to the dispersed geographical areas where this kind of education is most needed. We can't call on our regular teaching faculty because they already are carrying such heavy loads.

We must identify and recruit other capable people. These instructors are not always available where they're most needed, so we either have to transport them there or pay travel costs, which are expensive.

The problem isn't whether or not to provide up-to-date, current information; that's a given, that must be done. But the logistical obstacles that go along with that are formidable.

SUMMERS: Yes—for a number of reasons. You know, when library schools first began to have enrollment and costs problems, everybody jumped on the continuing education bandwagon thinking that was going to be a way to help solve that problem, and it hasn't.

There are some very fundamental reasons why not.

First, vendors of systems of various kinds have jumped in to provide a lot of continuing education.

Second, libraries have gotten smarter, and when they write contracts and specifications for systems, they write into them that the vendor will provide a relatively high amount of training so they get that as part of the package for their staffs.

Library schools have, of course, jumped in and are providing a fairly fundamental level of technical training as part of the M.L.S., so that that's already taken care of to some extent.

Also, we have a problem in that the institutions are always strapped for money. There's a limit to how much of their resources they can put into continuing education for their staffs. Librarianship's not a high-paying profession, so there's a limit to how much the staffs are going to reach into their own pockets to pay for it.

ASP: There hasn't been a widespread recognition by the organizations that employ librarians that they are going to have to make an investment in their people to retool them for change. Somebody once said to me, "We always get so busy dealing with the urgent that we don't have any time left to deal with the important." I think that's what's happened with continuing education. It gets a lot of lip service. People say, yes, it's important, but not much happens when it comes right down to asking is it worth two hours or four hours out of somebody's time a week?

How much is the organization going to invest in its budgetary resources, its staff time resources? It's always kind of gotten neglected there and not given the high emphasis or priority it should have. At the same time, I think maybe librarians, like a lot of other people, feel that they're stretched so thin they don't have time to pursue a lot of it on their own. So it's kind of fallen through the crack, unfortunately.

I hope that it can turn around so that there can be more emphasis and more support from the institutions and the organization in recognizing people as our major expense in operating libraries. To keep those people at the top skill levels, we're going to have to invest much more money.

STRONG: Continuing education has kept pace with the need in the library arena, yes. In some cases it's been very good.

Where it has missed the point is in the things that you wouldn't get through library continuing education, anyway. The change in our society, the change in the public policy arena, the change in management styles.

I'm not sure it's the responsibility of the profession to teach those things. I think it is our responsibility to be aware that they are needed and that we must be much more attuned to what's happening in government. But I'm not sure that's the responsibility of a library school or library continuing education to be teaching us.

What I don't see done well enough in library continuing education, frankly, is the update in the good basic service area—children's service, reference services, new resources. When you see those programs given—we did one this year on local history and genealogy resources at the state library conference—you have standing room only, because there's not that much of that kind of thing.

Individual professional development and the retooling and retraining we need to provide to run better libraries are two different issues in continuing education. I think we've over-emphasized and invested a lot of effort and money in the former area to the detriment of the improvement of library skills. I'm still one of those old hard-liners who thinks that the most important librarian is the one that's on the desk.

HEIM: Continuing education needs to explore other ways of delivery. It's becoming increasingly expensive for people to travel to a site and go to a conference, especially with such a high level of specialization that's become required.

I think that we will see an increase in the distant-learner concept, especially as promulgated by the folks at the University of South Carolina. We're experimenting at LSU with telelearning, broadcasting classes from one site to two or three other sites.

That may be a good way to get grass roots continuing education, as opposed to the travel to a conference.

WEDGEWORTH: Continuing education has been difficult because you need a critical mass of people who are in the immediate vicinity of the school in order to draw upon them adequately. The other reason it hasn't kept pace is our people get such strong programming through associations at a relatively low cost because they can aggregate the people at a given site. It's difficult to mount high-quality continuing education programs by the schools locally, because the price that we would have to charge for it would be out of proportion to the number of people who are available. If there were more people who were immediately available you could drop the price, but that's not the case even when you are in a major metropolitan area as we are.

In general, the associations, the Special Libraries Association, the Medical Library Association, the American Library Association and all of its divisions do a very fine job of continuing education. They do it primarily at conferences, but they also do it all year round. The Resources and Technical Services division, for example, has a wonderful series of traveling institutes that go all over the country year round. One or two days you get national faculty of international reputations who will come in for a workshop or an institute.

The price is relatively good, and they can generate a decent audience of 50, 60 people at a given site and justify the cost for the workshop or institute. The other associations emulate that. As a result, there's not as much pressure on schools to give more formal continuing education as there might be if our associations weren't doing such an effective job.

Should there be mandatory continuing education for first-class certification?

SUMMERS: The field has never sorted out how it feels about continuing education. Relatively few states or institutions have, except for school media specialists, any basic requirement that you have to have some amount of continuing education in order to continue to practice the profession, so there's no mandate for it.

Also, the reward system doesn't reward continuing education appreciably better than it rewards non-continuing education. So if you don't get any brownie points, you don't get any money points; therefore, the market hasn't developed.

If libraries and state certifying agencies and major academic institutions were to say, if you want to continue to work here you've got to get so much continuing education in a five-year period, then there would be a market for it.

ASP: Certainly other professions have gone the mandatory route. The medical profession requires continuing education, and the legal profession does, and the teachers have to go back every summer. I would think we would want that, too.

Yes, a part of being a professional and a practitioner in a profession is maintaining your knowledge. While there are a lot of people who are motivated to do it on their own and don't need some kind of a mandate to stimulate them, there are other people who do need the prodding.

The other thing mandatory continuing education might do for us is that it might help start building a recognition in the minds of the people who control our budgets that we're really important. We're just as important as the doctors and the lawyers and the nurses and the teachers. Society has recognized their need to keep their knowledge and skills current. As a consequence, then, we need the financial remuneration and the rewards for it, too.

Chapter 8

Censorship

This is all about how censors and censorship attack libraries. Will there be more or less? Will it come from the same sources or new fronts? What are the best ways for library leaders to fight back?

——— ♦ ♦ ♦ ———

How will censorship affect libraries of the future?

COOPER: We have special interest groups in this country and nutty people who get ego satisfaction from riding those horses off into the sunset.

Also, let's face it, this is a litigation-prone society now. It's getting evermore litigation-prone and people are going to bring suits just because they were turned down, because a book wasn't in the library when they thought it should be.

That is what I think the problem will be in the next decade. It will be nuisance suits filed by individuals and people who get pleasure out of asserting their rights.

How long this will continue depends on the political picture, on whether the political picture begins to swing back toward the norm from the ultraconservative views which were, in turn, a reaction to the very nice liberal climate that we enjoyed for so long. I hope we're ending our binge of repression of thoughts and ideas, and maybe beginning to swing back to a more normal mode.

STRONG: I think censorship is going to increase. The pressures are going to be by everybody.

Librarians have always been the most incredible of censors. We do it in what we select and how we provide access to what we don't select. I said I would never deny an interlibrary loan to something someone wants. But I engage in the highest form of censorship when I refuse to buy something, and I also refuse to borrow it if someone wants to read it. So we've got our own self to identify as a censor.

There are two other areas of censorship that bother me these days even more than intellectual, and they are economic and technological. Economic from the sense of the decreasing capability of libraries to capitalize, to buy the collection, to stay open, and to hire staff. And technological in our inability to capitalize and really provide improved access.

You watch it in the governmental sector, the growing amount of material that is in electronic formats. I am concerned that we really stand firm on the principles of privacy and confidentiality, and I say that in the context of us going through it in the state at the local level, increased pressures from local officials to know who's reading what. Our automated systems provide us with incredible power to do that.

A number of the libraries in the state are beginning to get such pressure. We've always had it, but with those old arcane manual circulation systems, it wasn't always easy to provide.

For example, a city manager who is not managing as well as folks thought he should one day finds on his desk books on management checked out of the local public library over which he has responsibility.

So he calls the librarian and says, "Who checked those out and who's being critical of my job performance?" and the librarian refuses to give him the record.

"I run the library. I'm responsible for the library. I have the right to see those records," he insists.

But does he? We thought that the state statute covered that. The statute requires a court order. That's what it says about the police, the courts. We're looking at that one very closely. What do we need to change in public privacy policy to protect this confidentiality?

It's a small town, probably no big shake to anybody, but I think it's a really serious indicator. Very serious indicator. And the city has lost a very talented professional. The city has come out on the short end of that one.

SUMMERS: I think there will be new groups coming along trying to restrict access. Or maybe it's simply that the society is more and more chopped up into sub-groups that people belong to and those sub-groups have different kinds of coalitions that they put together.

We realize that information is important, and who has it and who controls it and so forth is an important social issue not restricted to us alone. Other people have that realization, too.

For example, until relatively recently, we didn't have any particular conflict with the people who create and distribute information trying to get into our business, because they didn't deem that they could make a profit in it. Now there are many who think they can. Obviously, their desire would be to have us do less of what we do so they could do more of it. That's not censorship per se, but it begins to have an impact.

We also have a growing belief among people that they cannot do much about society—I can't control inflation, I can't do much about world peace, I can't do much about AIDS—but I can do something about the books my kid brings home from the library, and that's what I'm going to do.

Because people have these frustrations, we get an intensity of their focus on those things they can have some impact on, and censorship of library books is one of them.

ASP: Just the other night on TV there was a story about video cassettes on the local news. Parents were concerned about kids being able to get video cassettes that are more violent than the parents want to see or want their kids to see.

It's a continuum. And it's a kind of pendulum that swings back and forth, and I think we're going to go through periods again where there is more interest in censorship and more efforts to censor library collections. But then it seems like it swings back the other way, too. Communism and sex—they're always the things that get people riled up, and violence, too.

Right now what has most people concerned is sex-related things and particularly videos. Somehow that's so much more graphic when you can see it, rather than when you just read it. It's going to be a constant thing. We're always going to have to deal with it and always going to have to keep the vigil on.

One of the things we're recognizing in libraries is that we've got allies, and we're not fighting the censorship battle alone. Organizations like the state newspaper association share the same stance that we do on intellectual freedom and access to information. The broadcast media less so, but the print media are right there on the front line with us. We'll be in a better position if we cultivate some of those allies so they're alert to the problems that we have, and we're alert to the problems they have.

WISENER: We had sort of a flurry of problems. They seem to travel in little gaggles and they come trotting in with all these complaints and then there's silence for a while. Right now we have been in the silent period for a year at least.

I'm sure that there's always going to be a rebel and I'm sure there's always going to be someone who probably feels there aren't new worlds to conquer; they have to conquer something. I think they like to stand up and be heard and seen, but I don't see it escalating.

CHISHOLM: I think the conservative groups will multiply and move into a variety of areas. I believe conservative religious groups will proliferate. There will be an increase in the attempts at governmental control. All of these things will add to the problems of freedom of access and will increase censorship. Censorship-related problems will increase for adults, children, teenagers, everyone.

WHITNEY: I'm afraid I do see a greater effort to restrict minors for the next few years. The society becoming more and more conservative certainly has an impact on resources that are challenged in school libraries and in any other kind of library. Hopefully, by the time we reach the twenty-first century, our citizenry will realize that the ability to critically read and evaluate materials is a skill that all of us need if we are going to be able to think for ourselves. Then, ideally, censorship will cease to be a problem.

It seems that every year we have another group that appears out of nowhere to object for totally different reasons. For so many years, censorship was basically aimed at materials that were sexually explicit. That no longer seems to be the case. People object to materials for a variety of reasons, and I suppose those reasons will continue to change every year.

GORAL: Our best weapon as far as censorship is concerned is the public. As far as the braille *Playboy* incident was concerned, Congress was saying that this was a purely fiscal decision that needed to be made, and we said no, it's not, it's a matter of censorship. Why pick *Playboy* out of a dozen or two dozen other magazines?

We had people who stood behind us and it really was the people, the clients who use the service, who helped us win this case. A lot of letters written to people in Congress from clients who use this service saying, "Hey, you're taking away a decision that I have made as an adult to read this information and this is the format that I choose to read it in." The money was not the main problem here at all.

For years, sighted people have looked at blind people and said, well you should do this, or you shouldn't do that, you can do this or you can't do that. In this situation, again they felt this restraint by the sighted community saying, you shouldn't read this, saying "good" blind people shouldn't read *Playboy* magazine.

McDONALD: We have to be really careful about electronic censorship. If all the world's information ends up being in machine-retrievable form, how easy for a government who didn't like an ex-president to just globally remove him from the history books forever or to change other things forever. Librarians have to guard against that happening.

STEPANIAN: We haven't had the censorship problem.

Last year, one mother very proudly said that in another community she had gotten a particular book off the shelf. I alerted everybody to the fact that this was happening and when we talked with the mother and gave her all the forms she had to fill out, her only concern was, I don't want my sixth-grade student to read it.

That was no problem. The teacher worked with the youngster and said, "Your mother has asked that you not read any more books by this particular author." And that was all there was to that.

We had one experience with a Chinese family in which the youngster brought home a book on witchcraft and the parents objected. Again, the mother said, "I don't want him reading anything related to that," and it was easy to comply.

We only had one case, one book, that ever went through the whole process of being reevaluated by a community group and the school group and our whole policy. That was back in 1974–75. The consensus was that indeed this book should stay on the shelf. There was no reason why it should be off.

There were people recently who were very concerned with some of the AIDS materials that we had. Then we had one of our teachers diagnosed as having AIDS. Fortunately, the community came forward with support. The doctor at the Cleveland Clinic, who I learned was treating this particular teacher, came forward to help.

Every other doctor, male and female, within our district who found out what was happening immediately called the superintendent and said, this is my background, this is my specialty. If there's anything I can do to help, please let me know.

We had our regular all-school PTA scheduled so the community did have the chance to share the information. The teacher involved and the doctor at the Cleveland Clinic could not compliment the district highly enough for the way in which that whole situation was handled.

Parents want youngsters to know what's happening. Of course, you have to understand we have a highly educated group. The only question that came from a parent at that PTA meeting was from someone who did not have an education comparable to the other parents and who didn't have all the information, didn't understand that by touching you were not going to get AIDS.

We did a great deal of in-service with our staff. They were the ones who were highly concerned about what was going to happen. "Am I going to get it? If by emptying a wastebasket, am I going to have a problem?" And we've done two in-services with them. They were so appreciative that doctors came, that nurses came, that people were willing to answer their questions. So that fear was taken away.

EASTMAN: We seem to be getting more kooks in our society. Every day we're spinning off groups from the middle that have private agendas and think the rest of the world should be controlled, forced to wear their spectacles so as to see the world the way they do. We'll probably see more of that.

Targeting younger children is the easiest place for these people to start, and the best place to find them is in schools. Schools are easier to hit than libraries.

SMITH: Attempts to censor will always be with us. People have different values, and people like to think that their values are the one and only, or the best, or the important ones, or the real ones. And because of that we're always going to have differences. This last decade we've been through the whole fundamentalist, religious censorship issues.

Certainly at some point, with technology, we're going to be into the right-to-know kinds of issues and the government suppression and who should know that. The environmental issues. The defense. All of that is going to become so much more important because it's going to be available through databases and online sources.

There will always be something. It's up to the profession to assert the role of libraries and if the role is, as I believe, to see to it that information is made available to the people, then we have to be willing as leaders to be courageous and not be intimidated or forced to compromise.

One thing I don't see is a particular attempt to deny access to minors. Kids are exposed to more at a younger age through other sources and they're more mature at a younger age. Ten-year-olds and five-year-olds 20 years from now will have more information at a younger age. Hopefully, that means we can also deal with it better.

Information in and of itself is not dangerous. It's how we use it and what we think it means.

Chapter 9

The Dream Library

In this chapter we asked our library leaders to describe their
dream library of the late 1990s. Here they tell what visions
they have for a better world for both librarians and users.

———— ◆ ◆ ◆ ————

What's your dream for your library in 1998?

MASON: A major public library in an urban environment will
include a full range of services from branch level to research level.
It will have a branch system composed of small branches located
relatively close together, easily accessible to the communities that
they serve. Staff will be very friendly and helpful.

These branches will be connected to the main library so that
an individual can get virtually anything he or she wants through
that branch. In some instances, they can get it rather quickly
using telephone lines, facsimile transmissions. So that if someone
needs a relatively obscure article for a term paper and doesn't
want to or can't go downtown, they can in fact go into their
branch library and it can be FAX-ed out. It might be easier to do
that than to put it on a delivery truck.

The main library will have a relatively large collection, whatever formats those are in. The physical building itself will house a
range of materials. It will also link electronically to other libraries
around the world, not only around the country, but around the
world, and will be able to receive and send all kinds of information.

It will be quite sophisticated in its searching capability. It will
be more or less easy to use, although whenever you have a large
collection it begins to get complex, no matter what you do. We
have 2 million volumes in our main library, and close to 8 million
items when you consider everything in microfilm and microfiche.
There's no way to make that simple, but it can be easier to use
than it is now.

We will provide searches for businesses and have profiles for some businesses so we can routinely provide information for whoever signs up for that kind of service.

I want to see the public library as the information center for the community so that whenever anyone wants any kind of information, what they think of first is the library. The information there is as close as a telephone, as close as a computer.

We will have electronic delivery systems that will be routinely used. People will routinely be able to search the catalog just by dialing in and using their computers.

It's very important to have this available through the branches because we would normally provide it to people in their homes or offices if they have computers. But some people won't have them and won't have access to them. The branches then provide a very important service just from a philosophical point of view, because they will help us not become a nation of information rich and information poor.

People will continue to come into the library, but some will also be very heavy users of the library and never come into it. I find that the more services we provide that don't require people to come into the library, the more people come to the library. I find that astonishing. Our use at the main library in Cleveland increased 12% in the last quarter of the year 1987—and this was for a population that is declining.

The new technology doesn't appear to replace, it expands at every level, so I don't think that what we'll have in 10 years are buildings that are not used. I think we'll have buildings that are used more than they are now.

DOUGHERTY: I don't know what my dream library will look like, but I hope to create an environment where librarians are viewed by campus communities as true information providers. If we are going to enhance the roles of public service librarians on campus, these staff must be perceived as members of the academic team in terms of providing information either to students or faculty.

By 1998 I hope those who populate academic communities will more fully appreciate the importance of better access to collections and information as contrasted with today's emphasis on the availability of stand-alone local collections. Today ownership is viewed as being much preferable to access to remote collections, but as libraries become increasingly dependent on each other's collections, access services must assume greater importance.

To achieve this goal we must first put into place services that really do provide dependable and timely access to publications. Today's conception of what is timely and dependable is unacceptable to the majority of those who use libraries. We will need to rethink how access services can be better provided.

De GENNARO: New York Public Library is one of the two or three great libraries in this country. It came into existence in 1895. At that time the trustees had a vision of the future, both for the branch libraries and for the research library.

The research library came into existence because it was felt that the United States and New York City needed a library like the British Museum Library, and the Bibliotheque Nationale, and other European national libraries. If New York was to be a world class city, it needed a world class library resource. That was the vision.

The trustees hired John Shaw Billings to come and make it all happen. In Billings, the trustees got some very inspired leadership in the early part of the century. We have a saying here that Billings built the building, Anderson built the staff, and Lyndenberg built the collections.

I think we're standing on the shoulders of those giants and the distinguished trustees who guided this library in that formative period. They developed a vision of the future for the New York Public Library which stood it in good stead for its first century.

Our task now is to formulate a vision of the New York Public Library that is appropriate for its second century. I feel privileged to be a part of today's leadership along with Gregorian and our trustees. We have an extraordinary group of trustees, and we are riding a wave of popular support that these trustees and Gregorian have been able to generate.

Our job is to try to formulate a realistic vision for the twenty-first century as our predecessors did for the twentieth century. That new vision has to take into account the changing economic, social, and demographic scene in New York. That's the challenge.

It's not going to be easy and it won't be done quickly, but I think the future of the New York Public Library in the twenty-first century is going to depend on how well we integrate these branch and research functions of the library and how well we perform as a single library that serves the needs of all users. We start with preschool children, we catch them while they're young and impressionable, and then we go right on up the scale to the authors and the writers and so on.

New York is very special, because we have that whole constituency and New York is the intellectual and communications center of the country. So we not only have the capability, but we have the right audience. And if it can't be done in New York, I don't know where we're going to do it. We have a fantastic opportunity.

We also have our prime location. We have a symbolic location in mid-town Manhattan with a landmark building. The marble building with the two lions out in front. That says "library" to millions of people when they see that image, and we use that image a lot, our lions and the facade of our building.

Symbolically, it's a very important thing. Of course, that same building gives us problems. It's not a flexible building, but as a symbol it's absolutely fantastic.

Our research library is and is going to continue to be open to anyone who comes in to make use of our collections.

We ask no questions, we don't ask for letters of reference or recommendation, so that whatever we have is available on equal terms to anybody who walks in regardless of educational level or social class. It has been that way right from the start and will continue to be that way—without charge, without complications, without questions, without recommendations from authorities or other scholars, and so on.

This library, and perhaps the Library of Congress, are the only two real research libraries left in the United States where any member of the general public is allowed in.

Most of the university libraries, private as well as public, are making terms and conditions for use. Many of them charge fees to outsiders. I'm not criticizing that because they have to do it in order to effectively serve their primary users.

But nevertheless, we, the New York Public Library, and the Library of Congress, are the last of the free, openly available libraries.

BERGER: The communication problem which appears to exist between libraries and the rest of society will no longer exist. There's full and complete communication. People recognize why libraries are essential. They are willing to support those libraries which should be publicly supported.

Librarians, on the other hand, have become much more sophisticated about information in general and have stopped proclaiming that all information at all times should be free to all people. Why should the taxpayer support an IBM scientist working on a government contract who wishes to borrow 100 items from this library?

Libraries are after all the knowledge base and the corporate memory of this nation. When we talk about our national resources and defending them in times of emergency, we will talk not only about the kinds of things we defend now, but we will also talk about security for libraries because we will recognize that they represent the memory of this nation.

We will have solved most of our preservation problems. They're not all that formidable, actually. They seem so only because we've been an impoverished profession in the past, but that will change in the best of all worlds.

ROSENTHAL: One of the major considerations is a physical plant that constitutes the tangible context for offering good service, which I find is a decided lack at Berkeley and something that we're trying to do something about. It's a long, slow process.

That is terribly important because it not only provides a context to offer good service on site, it influences the emotional and psychological aura for both users and staff that helps make the information process a positive rather than a negative experience.

It also, in the best of all possible worlds, provides a physical situation that is amenable to change. We're undergoing what for us in libraries is a series of very rapid changes, and the physical plant often times impedes those changes and our ability to cope with the changes.

I hope that in 10 years we will have accomplished a major goal for our library which will be retrospective conversion of all our bibliographic records. And some conversion of records that we're not now actively contemplating to convert, such as more extended bibliographic access into our 50 million-piece manuscript collection.

GORAL: When people see our library building, they are going to think, gosh, I'd like to go into that, it looks really interesting. It looks like something dynamic is happening inside.

Inside, we'll have hardware and software available for anyone, any print-handicapped person, to come in and use. We'll have individuals there who will be familiar with that hardware and software so they can help anyone who is not all that familiar with it.

We'll be able to provide materials to our clients quickly.

We'll personify a real positive image that says we are a good and fine organization.

We'll have materials and equipment that work and meet the needs of our clients. We won't be putting our clients a step behind the individual who can read print materials.

We'll be the same as the public library as far as materials are concerned, as far as the reference services that are available, as far as technology is concerned.

I guess I don't see the salaries changing all that much in the 1990s. I think, traditionally, we've sat back and we've said, okay, we are not as important as other services. We have this subliminal feeling about ourselves that we're not as important as other organizations in the community and we have to wipe that out and say, yes, we are. And we deserve to be paid as much as any professional.

Mind drain sometimes is much more strenuous than physical drain.

WHITNEY: I have a vision of this beautiful school library with bright colors, with lots of plants, lots of open space, lots of windows, although that's been unrealistic in a school library with lots of equipment because of security reasons, but we'll say we paint wonderful scenes on walls that approximate windows. A very, very busy place with lots of students and lots of teachers engaged in a variety of activities.

My ideal library on my campus would have three classes busily engaged in different kinds of activities. Students doing online searching. Students using the *Oxford English Dictionary*, looking at word etymology and enjoying it. Students in a computer lab working on a science project using microcomputer software.

Copy machines of the future will cost a penny a sheet. Copy machines will enlarge 20 times, reduce 20 times, and will print in color. You can produce transparencies with them.

There will be special viewing places for kids to use whatever the latest technology is—a new kind of VCR that we can't dream of yet. Perhaps the laser disk will come into its own.

The library will be totally automated. Public access catalogs. Circulation totally automated. Book detection systems will be unobtrusive. I don't think we'll ever get away without them, but they will be convenient.

Microforms will be common and easily available with storage that's convenient; microform machines will be much easier to use, and copies from microforms will be much cheaper.

Probably a lot more microfiche. We're buying more and more microfiche, so I would assume that we will continue to do that unless there's another major development; perhaps microdot will be big in the 1990s.

Our remodeled facility will have a teacher work room right off the library reading room. It will be fully equipped with microcomputers, with reproduction equipment, with a letter press, with file cabinets, book shelves, and nice space for teachers to do their lesson preparation.

The teachers will use the library as an office and a planning center, for department meetings, inter-department meetings. The library will be the information hub of the school.

All students will use the library because it will be absolutely essential. The curriculum of the 1990s will contain a whole strand of information skills. Not a separate curriculum, but interspersed throughout the required curriculum so that we insure that all students, regardless of what their intentions are following graduation, will develop the skills.

The development of information skills in the past has been rather haphazard, depending upon what teacher students had; we want to insure that we have identified the skills that are absolutely essential for students to access and use information successfully in the next century. We want to make sure that those skills are developed through the required courses, so we are not adding anything to what students already must take, and that we just deliver the information through already required curriculum.

The librarian will be an integral part of the total school, of the whole instructional process. Everything that goes on in the school will relate in some way to the library media program, whether it's the use of materials in the center, or that are accessed through the center in the classroom, or whether the activities take place in a library media center. Everything will connect through the library.

The principal still will be one of the few persons who has more impact than a librarian. The principal is the key. The principal sets the tone. The principal establishes the expectations. The principal is the instructional leader and will always have the most impact.

In addition, the custodian always has a great deal of impact on what happens. The kids can't learn if the room is too cold or the room is too hot. If the chalkboards aren't cleaned, the custodian is the culprit.

On the broader front, as we move into the next century there is not going to be as much of a distinction as there currently is between librarians depending upon where you work.

The school librarian has been in a quandary trying to really decide where our real home is. Are we librarians first or are we teachers first? And that's been a major point of discussion in the profession which we see reflected in the American Library Association, which unfortunately has never paid a great deal of attention to the preparation of school librarians.

In the 1990s, I see school librarians beginning to work much more closely with public librarians and the special librarians as we recognize the need to use resources from a variety of places. But I suppose that teaching background and our strong ties with the instructional process will continue to set us apart in some ways from librarians in other types of institutions.

STEPANIAN: I see the school library well-staffed in order to give service.

I see teachers being extremely involved in the library resources, their planning being done with library materials and not with textbooks.

I see curriculum guides that they have written, and I see them using various media for what their youngsters are doing.

I also see that they may have a youngster at fifth grade, for example, a very high achiever and a very bright youngster, studying some of the same things as other youngsters working at the national norm (which is low for us in our district), but being able to achieve and being satisfied with what they are doing within the library.

I see the constant flow of classes coming in with the teacher and doing what it is they need to do.

We talk about the library being the core, the center of everything. I really mean that. I don't mean just physically being there, but the library playing a major role. That if, indeed, that library were to be closed and we were to do away with librarians and all the support staff within the libraries, the teachers would have a revolution. They would be up in arms and they would protest.

I see money being no problem. Materials will be available whenever and wherever. If you want a book, you can have it tomorrow. If you want a film, a video, whatever, you'll have it tomorrow. It will be easy access to whatever it is that person needs.

I see databases in the building. I'd love to be able to see a database built just for children.

When I need a review on a particular micro software, I'll be able to see a database I can just dial in and access immediately and pull up three reviews.

I would like to be able to have a database of all our materials so that if Fernway School needed more materials on, let's say the holocaust, they could see that the high school and a few other places have those materials and they could immediately call them in and the next day make them available within their building.

We'll have closed-circuit access through video throughout our whole district so our board meetings can be televised. Certain important speakers at the high school may be of value to one class at one other school, so instead of transporting the youngsters all over the city, we can give them TV access to this national figure right in their own classrooms.

ASP: In 10 years the agency will be a real crucial information-switching center to which state government knows it can turn for information real fast.

It's going to be a place that the library community throughout the state can realize is their advocate in government. It's the folks who are doing the forecasting, the trend identification, the issue identification, the long-range planning. It's the people that are developing and implementing the structures for the library profession so that the services are up to date.

Are libraries really all that different than they were 10 years ago? They don't look all that much different in terms of the building. But we have added a lot in that time—all the video cassette activity, and we're getting into compact disks for audio recordings. It seems like any new format for recording information that comes along for the consumer market finds its niche in libraries. It's generally an add-on; it's not something that replaces something else.

One of the immediate problems that I hope by 1998 we've got a better handle on is the mentality that we don't want to tax ourselves for anything. The best government is no government and the best tax is no tax, such people think, and by 1998 I hope we're back to the point where we can recognize that there are certain public investments that have to be made, that the public has to pay for, and that library information services is one of those that's so basic it's a crucial public investment of public money.

It's been a tough decade. Libraries have hung on, but it hasn't been easy; we've had to spend a lot of time and effort trying to counter that notion.

EASTMAN: There will be a lot more service to people who are not able to leave home. We are a graying society. Services to the handicapped and housebound, to those in nursing homes, hospitals, and prisons will improve. Such library service is generally inadequate at present, and it is mostly under-funded.

DUMONT: The futurist Robert Smith wrote an article in the '70s which stated that during the next two decades most libraries will evolve into information centers where work stations and librarians will be interacting with you on a one-to-one basis and helping you get the information you want by using video display machines from a computerized database.

What will it be like in 1998? There will be more one-to-one interaction and there will be a specialist for the types of information resources that are available. Books will be there, but there will be much more up-to-date computerized information available online. We're going to be answer people, we're going to be answering people, we're going to find information in whatever resource we can. I see a greater portion of databases. You'll be able to go to one source to get information on almost anything. We will be interpreters of questions as we always have been. We'll be guides to the users. Our reference questions will be more sophisticated and we will develop tools to gain answers. We in the tech services area will continue to harness this data into a logical format and to provide information to the users. I hope that we'll have done away with all the barriers of resource sharing. We will be specialists in lots of ways, but we will be able to exchange information in machine-readable form and in a very quick format, whether it's microwave or some other telecommunications technology. There will be no barriers to what we can provide our users. But we'll have to be ever so cognizant of the danger of providing old data. We're always going to need a level of quality control on the data we provide our users, as we do today, as perhaps we should do more today. Right now we let the user beware in some areas.

We will provide information to the users in whatever format they need it, whether it's on a diskette or a little card that you carry in your pocket with a memory chip.

We're going through, if not a revolution, certainly an evolution toward sophistication of using many technologies that until now we have not been able to use, perhaps because we have such mammoth databases, such mammoth data to control that we must spend all of our energies trying to find a way to control it.

In 1998 that will not be the case. We'll be able to share knowledge and bibliographic information without regard to bureaucratic walls or technical barriers.

What's your dream for library trustees in 1998?

WISENER: I'd like library trustees to be very aware of their community needs, to be aware that they speak for the population, not themselves. To be even-tempered and listen to ideas other than their own. That's a problem that exists so often in boards: when there's trouble, it's because there is no compromise.

I'd like them to be representative of many areas. We tend to have thinking-alike and members of about the same age, because that's when people have time for this kind of service. We need a lot more young people.

Being named a trustee no longer is the little gift that they give to the good citizen who has worked and done a lot of community service. That used to be where the board people came from. I think you need more youth than we have now in the American Library Trustee Association or in any local board.

I would like to see all boards with the most marvelous orientation program because if there isn't a good orientation program, new members are useless for a long time. It's a shame to have that standing-still time. We should have everything from the by-laws to a tour of the library. Follow a new book all the way through technology, be really aware of every program in the library. We need this in at least six two-hour sessions, because too much too fast and you aren't going to absorb it.

I would like trustees to be active locally so that they do know what's going on in the community. I would like to see them active statewide, because that brings a picture of the state and the state laws and what needs to be done in that area. And the most educational thing I've ever done was to become active nationally, too. I learned there that the problems that you think exist only in your world exist everywhere.

The perfect trustee has to be a very well-rounded person.

I'd like them to be able to speak publicly. Some of them are going to want to do that, and those are the best voices to be out there. I would like them to be willing to be advocates, to be willing to stand up and be counted, whether politically or socially.

In today's library world, trustees represent not only citizens who are legally responsible for libraries in many states, but they are also the hope for financial growth and enhancement of public awareness. Legislators at all levels are responsive to citizen action. We trustees either are the "movers and shakers," or we have access to them. I look for a growing association between librarians and their lay supporters, including Friends of the Libraries, along with trustees.

My hope for libraries in the next decade is that trustees will play an active role in the continuing trend toward diverse, not limited, thinking and service. I think they will, knowing the depth of their commitment.

COOPER: Trustees should be leaders of the community, people who are helping minority groups, people concerned with raising educational levels in the community. And people who can do something for the library with the political body, but who also have management expertise or other expertise that can be used by the library.

I think that they should not be concerned with the operations of the library, except to represent the needs of the user in its policies and activities. I think they should be more concerned with getting funding, promoting public use, and representing the library.

It's essential that the board be a broad-based group and that every effort be made to see that the new immigrants to our country be represented, as well as existing groups trying to raise their standard of living.

Also, there's got to be an even more concerted effort to bring youth in. That's not so easy. Once after the White House Conference, we had a high school student on our board. The poor kid was so busy with basketball and everything else.

The trustees ought to get the public library closer to the schools. There's been the area of school libraries and the area of public libraries and while they know each other, the cooperation has not been as close as it will have to be in the next decade.

For example, we started with literacy programs. Now we have this national library card business. The Library of Congress sponsored a meeting at one time, maybe five years ago, where they talked about the public library, school library, and home partnership. With this tremendous change in our society, they're all going to come together and they're just going to have to develop a closer relationship, as we have in our county.

One of our regional libraries is on a community college campus. We're planning that another will be connected with a school, and, in addition, our main library is also the downtown university library. Now that type of partnership ought to be extended to eliminate overlapping, and also to make people feel more comfortable with using all types of libraries at different stages in their lives.

Chapter 10

Leadership

This is a major exploration of many facets of leadership—what makes a leader, what leadership techniques work best, how a newcomer to the library field best learns how to become a leader, how library associations can encourage more leadership development, what new skills and attributes the library leader must have by 1998, and more.

———— ♦ ♦ ♦ ————

What made you a leader?

WEDGEWORTH: In this field, leadership is not so heavily dependent on personal characteristics, but on understanding how things get done. There are not too many one-man or one-woman shows in librarianship, because the field is grounded on elaborate cooperative and collaborative ventures.

Those persons who tend to do well in our field are able to get their work done through others and are able to keep focused on specific objectives and not get lost in the most current fad or the most popular direction.

They are the ones who are willing to ignore conventional wisdom in terms of looking at a problem and trying to strike out in a different direction. But mostly it comes down to very fundamental kinds of behavioral characteristics that tend to help you develop influence. And I distinctly emphasize influence, because there are very few power opportunities in our field.

My view of the way you develop influence is through continuity, reliability, being able to understand what other people want and how that can help you achieve what you want. If you can satisfy their wants in the course of achieving what you want, then you've built the next step to where you want to go.

Understanding the difference between power and influence is the key to success in our field. Not very many things are done directly, where you can simply order that it be done.

Sure, you can do minor things within a given institution where you have the power to hire and fire employees, but it doesn't get you very far.

Mostly it's a matter of developing extensive relationships, being able to work effectively with committees, but at the same time, being able to assert initiative and to state an unpopular position and back it up and get some adherents to pursue that particular position.

But the leadership in our field revolves around the ability to lead in collaborative arrangements, to persuade people to follow a particular course of action, and to get the work done through others.

I learned that in my very early training in the library field. When I came into the field there were seven or eight jobs for every graduate librarian, and it was possible to move up very quickly into very responsible positions.

I had good advice from a number of mentors so that I resisted that temptation just to take a bigger job, and I chose my developmental positions very carefully so that by the time I got to be a library manager, I knew virtually every basic job in a library, and I could do every basic job in the library. So when I talk about libraries I feel fairly confident that I know from personal experience and supervision precisely what goes on. That's one aspect of it.

I had pretty good training in early management, because most of my early management focused on handling people. I've also had some bad times. I remember the first time I got a major assignment to reorganize a department. I ended up turning a woman's desk to the wall; she came in and took one look and spent the rest of the day in the ladies' room crying because I had isolated her from her colleagues.

It was a simple lesson that you can't learn very easily from a textbook, dealing with those kinds of things.

I had lots of opportunities, but mostly my training as a manager focused on people.

How to interview them, how to identify the good performers, how to motivate people to be productive, and how to avoid getting involved in decisions in which management has no stake are basic. Many decisions that relate to personal style and certain working conditions that workers can always find ways to figure out for themselves and in which management has no stake are the pitfalls of management decision making.

It takes a certain amount of discipline to avoid being drawn into every question. When do you have the Christmas party? What difference does it make to management? You know you're going to lose a certain amount of time during certain times of the year and what is convenient for the employees is probably best for the organization.

So those kinds of things I thought were very helpful to me, of course, because most of the money in libraries is tied up in people.

If you're not effective in handling people, you won't be effective in handling the operation. We have not done the best job in our schools in training librarians to handle personnel. This is one of the areas that we will have to strengthen in our curriculum for the next decade.

When I look around at people who are leaders, I find different types. I find leaders like Henriette Avram who have superior technical understanding and knowledge that you have to respect. She combines that with an ability to work in a broad range of cooperative and collaborative contexts, both nationally and internationally, and her technical knowledge and understanding puts her head and shoulders above most of her contemporaries.

Then you have people who understand organizations and know what makes organizations work, and they're very good at directing organizations to achieve broad goals over longer periods of time.

Then of course you have those who are very good at identifying, selecting, attracting, and hiring good people. They train them and send them out into more responsible positions.

Understanding technology, understanding organizations, understanding people are the key areas in which leadership manifests itself.

BERGER: Curiosity, I guess. I wanted to be a veterinarian. I was adopted and my foster father, who was a dentist, said no woman in his family would ever go to med school because "you'd just get married and have kids."

So I left home and got a job in a library. It was at a time when computer technology was obviously going to change everything libraries did and I knew it.

It was also a time when certain facets of science—genetics for one, plasma physics for another—were just taking off and I was privileged in those days to work with top people in these fields. It was just so exciting, it never occurred to me to do anything else.

Working as a science librarian has taxed my physical and mental abilities to their utmost. I can't imagine a more satisfying career.

I did take the time later on to get the M.L.S. and I loved the experience. Betty Stone was my mentor and the reason I enjoyed it was because I had to make the time to think through what I'd been doing and why I'd been doing it. That was a very satisfying experience. I'm glad I didn't get that degree earlier. I'm glad I had the number of years I had working and managing scientific libraries beforehand, because I think I got more out of the experience.

VASILAKIS: First of all, I loved what I did in the library. I absolutely was excited about what I was doing. Being a part of what was happening in the corporation was important to me, and so I made it my business to find out what was going on and how could I get involved.

For example, we were involved in litigation that was a crisis for Westinghouse. The day after that suit was announced, our executives had on their desks, in their mail, a compilation of all the newspapers and all the articles that dealt with Westinghouse and the suit.

It's that kind of thing. That immediate. Let's get it out there. That's what they're going to ask us for so let's get it out there before they even ask. Being proactive, not reactive.

We were anticipating the need and providing the answers before the questions were asked. And nothing must ever be too much trouble to do. Nothing. Ever. I don't want to hear someone say, well I can't do that because I have to do this. Our customers don't want to hear that.

If someone asks us for something, we just do it. You don't go into a song and dance about how long it's going to take or how complicated it is. Customers shouldn't be bothered with that. Your job is to get it to them.

There's a lot of satisfaction in giving people what they want. That's a tremendous reward for me; what really turns me on is to give somebody something they want and they're really happy.

It's so easy to get good feedback in a library. Really, when you think about it, librarians can do very little wrong. You have an opportunity in the special library to really make a difference, you really do.

It's so easy to make a difference if you really want to. You get the same users time and time again. The people who used to be users in my library when I first started out are now vice presidents and beyond. It's nice to be able to know the top echelon up there, know them by first name. Because I knew them when. And they remember that the library has always been there when they needed it.

HEIM: There's just so much to be done, and I have a tremendous fear that I won't get a lot done. The ideas seem to just keep coming, and I just can't seem to stop trying to want to complete them. Just always having 15 things that I have to accomplish. I don't know why. I wake up each morning hoping I can inch up a little bit on each of them but they seem to keep adding on. I don't know, just a desire to finish things. New ideas seem to spring from old ones.

McDONALD: I really don't know. I guess I love this field. I was a substitute teacher and I was also substituting in libraries. Every time I was at a library I'd always redo it mentally. I'd think, how would I do it better if I were here? What was really good about it, what wasn't, and what could be improved?

Very early on, I liked and understood automation. I took the first course at Stanford in computer programming when I was a graduate student in economics. I've always known what computers can do for libraries and certainly libraries are a natural for automation.

I have a vision for our library, and I am always moving toward it. I believe in myself and always find a way to accomplish my goals.

SUMMERS: I had to develop it. I had a lot of help in doing it. I had mentors along the way who steered me to the kinds of experiences that enabled me to do it. Maybe because of a family circumstance and upbringing, I had an uncommonly large desire to do it, high motivation.

I can remember having trembling knees and churning stomach when I had to stand up and talk to a group of people. I can remember being uncertain and hesitant and injecting myself into social situations that had the potential to be useful. We all do that and the difference is that it's a learned skill.

I don't believe that leaders are born. They choose to be leaders and they seek out those kinds of experiences which enable them to develop those abilities.

Now certainly, any of us at any time can be in situations in which we are thrust into leadership positions by contextual factors and we rise to that.

But I'm talking about people who consistently seek out leadership roles. I think they probably have a desire and motivation and it's shaped like any other psychological desire or motivation.

STRONG: I got my best management training when I was 16 years old and my grandfather in a saw mill said, "You're going to run the lumber yard this summer." I had seven, 50-plus-year-old men under me. I learned more about management then and learned that I had to do the work right along with everybody else, that I couldn't sit and philosophize. That was the greatest lesson I learned anywhere along the way.

I care a lot about what I do. I'm not afraid to get in and do some of it. I'm also not afraid to have very high expectations for the people with whom I work. I try to reward them when they achieve in their own right because that's my achievement, too. I also try to give them support to get there. I think also that I do have a little bit of vision in terms of where I want to see libraries.

That question of leadership is always difficult, because I think all of us are leaders in our own ways. Many choose to lead by doing nothing and that's their example. Others, and I hope I'm in that category, choose to lead by doing something, and that by carefully selecting what it is they do, by clearly speaking out about the direction the library should take, learn and grow.

I had good mentors early on in this profession who helped me have the patience to build. I started in this profession under a high school English teacher working in the high school library. She gave me the love of libraries, of books, of reading, of literature, very early on.

Throughout undergraduate school I had the luck of working with a couple of university administrators and of bugging them long enough and asking enough questions that I worked in every department in that library. Probably got my best library training that way.

I received an LSCA scholarship for graduate school and had the good fortune of ending up with Wally Bonk at the University of Michigan as my mentor.

One of the requirements of the LSCA scholarship was to return to Oregon and work for two years in a public library. Well, I walked right in as director in a small city library at Lake Oswego and worked for a city manager who had been assistant director of the California League of Cities and the National League of Cities. He had come there to start their council/manager form of government and retire after that. He was 60 and an incredible man.

I intended to stay a couple of years and move on, but stayed there seven years to watch that town grow from about 8,000 to over 20,000. I learned about local government in ways I never could have learned anywhere else.

I then went to Everett, Washington, and there learned that community was where it was all at because we had no money, and yet I never got a budget cut, I never laid anybody off. We expanded hours, we expanded programs, we really did things.

When the gas crisis hit we ran hot lines, recorded hot lines in 1976 before dial-in anything was something anybody talked about at the library. We would check with the gasoline dealers in the morning, and we would record what stations would be open what time of day.

I was able to go on to the Washington State Library during the formative days of the Washington Library Network, and boy, did I learn library politics in a state that was being forced to really assess for itself what its involvement with technology was going to be. I also learned in that job as deputy director that I didn't want to work for somebody else. I had a good boss, luckily, who really let me have a lot of latitude. But I'd been a director of a library eight years by that time. That really taught me a lesson, that I wanted to work in a leadership role that was at the top.

My biggest weakness was not realizing early enough in my career that everything wasn't possible. I think that gave me some years of spinning wheels, of trying to do too many things, but it also taught me to choose much more carefully and to not have undue expectations of staff, and I think that is one of the most critical issues of leadership. You can have the ideas, but you also have to have the talent to select people around you who have the same sense of vision, and who are willing to do the day-to-day work of carrying things out. Because in a job like mine you're on every waterfront.

You have to have people, to surround yourself with staff and with supporters who share your sense of vision. For example, if it weren't for the 63 public librarians who are really committed to performing literacy services, the California Literacy Campaign wouldn't work. That's just blunt reality. Whatever I could claim as achievement would be very hollow because we wouldn't be teaching anybody to read.

One of the biggest and the hardest things is to select ideas and forward thrusts that others can buy into and then let them do it and let them achieve it, and let them take their own piece of the glory along with the process. I wasn't always too skilled in holding back in my own enthusiasm of the moment. I don't know that I have improved at sharing that limelight with others, the rewards with others. I mean it's very gratifying, a little kid from northern Idaho to be playing in the arenas that one can play in on this kind of a job.

What leadership techniques do you find work best for you?

STEPANIAN: Involving everybody, and getting to know people, getting them to trust you in lots of ways, and serving them in various ways.

If you're one of our patrons and you ask for something, the turn around is very fast. For example, a couple of years ago, despite our very fine professional collection, I began to see that principals and other administrators were not interested in reading books. They didn't have time for that. What they really wanted was something quick that they could read fast, that they could quote, that would give them a good background on some subject they were investigating. So I enlarged the professional collection and I spent a great deal of money on journals.

I also found, because we were online with OCLC, I could do more research for them. If they were on a curriculum committee, sometimes I would hear that something was happening and I would casually mention, well, gee, I'll do an ERIC search for you. Or would you like more information?

Now it is just expected that the first thing they do is they call me—"I'm starting a committee, send me whatever you have" or "I need to do something on multicultural education."

Journals used to be just routed. The September issue would never get to somebody until May. I would go to pull something off the shelf to copy an article and it wouldn't be there, and that was so frustrating.

There had to be a better way, so I wrote all the administrators and said, these are all the journals and newsletters we subscribe to. For the journals, I will send you the table of contents of any you would like. Then I will send any specific article you would like. The newsletters I route, and they're pretty good about sending those around fast.

I just got a note from a new administrator, a new principal, and he said, "I like this service." People who leave the district say,

"I miss that service." It is like continuing education for them; it keeps them updated.

That's one way to involve people and have them realize the importance of a professional collection. I also advise the librarians to do the same thing in their building with their teachers.

DUMONT: I am a great believer in people power and people knowledge.

It's very important that you establish credibility among your colleagues. I happen to work in a system where interaction with others is extremely important. I'm very dependent on others and they are dependent on me. I interact with seven presidents, seven vice-presidents of instruction, seven vice-presidents of student affairs, a vice-chancellor of academic affairs, a vice-chancellor of business affairs. And that's just in the upper echelon structure. On a day-to-day basis I deal with seven deans of educational resources, seven directors of libraries, and a multitude of other professional staff, as well as faculty.

Communication and trust are extremely important. You have to establish a trust and a base with your people or you're dead in the water. Too many people have been isolated by their colleagues, by the people they work with and for, because they lack the kind of skill to communicate effectively with others. That's probably the most important leadership trait.

I also believe in allowing people to grow, in allowing people to make mistakes to grow. Once they've made mistakes and learn from their mistakes they gain more confidence and become far better employees and far better risk-takers. We must continue to be risk-takers, within reason. That's an important trait in leadership, to allow people to take a risk, to support them when they make mistakes, let them grow and allow them to give input.

If you allow people to clearly communicate their fears without being threatened, allow them an opportunity to grow, and take your time to hold their hand, or let them hold yours, you will find that you are able to go through change together.

A leader must have knowledge, but a leader also must be able to foster an environment of change and an environment of allowing people to take risks without threat.

HEIM: Having ideas that looked like they couldn't be accomplished and trying to accomplish them and bringing together a team of people to help me do it. Just not being afraid to have ideas.

For example, at Louisiana State University we have a double master's that our students gain in computer science and library information science. That was particularly difficult to implement because computer science requirements are so different from library science requirements. So we've been running around the Southwest identifying students in computer science departments who will come to our program.

BERGER: I delegate until I find I can't delegate any more. I want to give anybody who works for me as much as they can handle. I will give a person an assignment. If they need training I'll be sure they get that, and then I'll leave them alone to get the assignment done.

My reputation is that I'm very fair but I'm also very tough, and I am. If I've asked you to do something and it hasn't been done to my satisfaction, and we've talked about it, and we straighten it out, don't come back later with the same goof. Just don't. I try—and have succeeded, I believe—in being fair.

There are people who won't work for me because I am tough to work for. I'm hard on myself and I'm hard on other people. One of the things I like best about this Bureau is that it expects perfection from its staff.

WHITNEY: You can't lead if no one's willing to follow. When you assume a leadership position, one of your first responsibilities is to listen. You do the best you can to hear what's being said, to use it, to make the best judgments you can, and to build consensus as you go along. You can't lead if people don't want to go where you want to take them. So it's a process of building consensus.

And you have to have a vision. You have to know where you think people need to go, but you're not going to get them there if you can't convince them that's where they need to go. You never end up exactly where you thought you were going, because during the process of building consensus you shift your focus slightly, but if you're a leader, the key is to convince others.

DOUGHERTY: I just do my thing. I do have visions of where I want the library to go. I express those visions. I do my best to convince the staff. Sometimes I'm successful, sometimes I'm not.

I am a risk-taker—I know that—that's my style. There's no doubt about it.

I'm a pretty good campus politician. I'm now more interested in what I see happening in the 1990s. In order to implement my dreams for the next decade, I will need several million dollars. I don't have the money, but the prospect of what could be done is what turns me on.

I was also very fortunate in having worked for three people (I didn't know what "mentor" meant at the time) who helped shape my career. They let me do my thing and weren't afraid to let me fall on my face from time to time. They allowed me to make my mistakes; when they occurred, they picked me up, dusted me off, and sort of pushed me back in the fray. My mentors were Ralph Shaw, Jerry Orne, and Ralph Ellsworth.

I was Ralph Ellsworth's deputy at the University of Colorado for five years. Ralph let me run the library; he only asked that I keep him informed so that he would not be blindsided by faculty. In a way I've been administering university libraries for over 20 years.

I have an intense interest in mentoring. That's one of the reasons for our residency program at Michigan because I recognized after the fact the full impact my mentors had on my career. I would not have advanced into positions I held had they not prepared me and given me the opportunity to gain experience. They were leaders.

SMITH: I've been in a leadership role because I was thrust into it in many ways. And part of that was because my background has been that of a Mexican American, and I was the first Mexican American to do many things.

So coming into a profession like this at a time in history when people were concerned about the changing society thrust me into a leadership role. I was the only Mexican-American librarian for many years. The only one to have an M.L.S. At one time, the only one in public library service. Eventually there were three of us in the country, and I was the youngest.

At the time, the late '60s and '70s, there was a great deal of turmoil and examination, and I was a part of it and I haven't stopped being part of it. Even as director of Orange County Public Library, I have a concern for those social values and I have a social responsibility that my generation has. I don't see a lot of activism among new librarians; there wasn't much of it with the old librarians.

I think my generation had a sense of entering this profession for what we could do for others. So that thrust me because of all these other circumstances into a position where I was involved. I was asking ALA to do certain things, take on certain projects, recruitment, publishing in certain areas, collection development, whatever. That doesn't generally happen unless somebody's out there leading the way. I happened to be one of those early people. So I still do that and I still have that concern.

As for leadership techniques, you have to be vocal and confident. And you certainly have to be pretty good because leaders don't last long if they're not competent. You have to be willing to say things or stand up in front of a group that may not like what you have to say. Most decisions that have a long-term impact require that. They're not easily accepted either because they're new or they're uncomfortable or people just don't want to listen to them.

And you've got to be strong enough to expose yourself to whatever the reaction is. You can't be a leader without an inner strength, some inner characteristics. If you don't have those, you're not going to be a leader for long, or you're going to be a superficial one without any depth. They don't last long. You have to have that basic character, a strength and confidence and some ability to compromise. You can learn some of it, but the courageous stuff, I think you're born with that. You exhibit that throughout your life in all areas.

GORAL: I like working along with my staff. I like working with people, rather than having people work under me. There are so many more things that we can get done if we work together as a team.

I also like getting myself involved in other libraries. For instance, I'm part of an administrative unit of the Colorado State Library, so I'm involved in aspects of librarianship other than just the Library for the Blind and Handicapped.

That keeps me fresh, keeps me looking at what's going on, at technology and developments in other libraries, not only special but public and school. It encourages me to talk to other individuals who may have a different and a fresher perspective about a problem that I may be facing.

FARBER: I was lucky in coming to this institution and initially succeeding someone who wasn't very good. So I was regarded right away as a success. That kind of honeymoon period permitted me to do some things that were, admittedly, very good and different, and also to help me shape a staff. That put the library on the map, so to speak.

Then I had a good sense of public relations; there's no doubt about that. I was committed to showing the rest of higher education what we were doing here, because I thought what we were doing here was important. I took advantage of all kinds of public relation events—writing things, having workshops, speaking in various kinds of groups.

So I'm not sure that it was a matter of leadership as much as it was just taking advantage of various opportunities as they came along. Making some opportunities, to be sure, but taking advantage of them, making the most of them.

Two books were very influential in my career, not necessarily for leadership but very important for my learning. One was Guy Lyle's book on *The President, the Professor and the College Library*, a little book that I use and quote frequently. It's a very small book but has lots of very good advice.

The other one is *Teaching with Books*, by Harvey Branscomb. It came out in 1941. It was a joint publication I think of the Association of American Colleges and the American Library Association. Branscomb, who was director of the library and professor of early Christian literature at Duke University, took on the AAC project of finding out why students in colleges didn't use the library that much.

I didn't really appreciate that book until maybe about 15 years ago, after I came to Earlham, and realized that in some way I must have read it before, or certainly got the ideas before, because he said so many things that I had said myself. For instance, "The library is not an end in itself. The library is there to serve the institution."

Also, the fact that I had done graduate work before I went into library work gave me an insight into scholarship that I think a lot of librarians don't have.

Being in a Ph.D. program permitted me to understand how scholars think and work and the problems that they have, and actually having taught a couple of years on the college level also gave me some insight into the problems of teaching.

One of the experiences I had was when I was teaching here at Earlham a section of humanities. Part of my responsibility was to give instruction in using the library. I gave that instruction to all the other sections, but I forgot to give it to my own section. Why did I forget to give it to my own section? Because I was so busy with grades, preparing the next day's lecture, thinking about a text for the next term. That made me realize that no matter how much

I push instruction in library use, I have to realize that it's not the most important thing to most teachers. Their classes are and it's very easy for librarians to forget that, how important teaching is to a good teacher and that we can't leave it up to them to say, yes, I think the library is important. We have to keep reminding them of it, and they'll say, "Oh, I forgot about that."

But we can't depend on them. We have to respect the fact that their teaching is the most important thing and that they won't think of the library as the most important.

How does a newcomer in the library field best learn how to become a leader?

STRONG: You have to be convinced that you're in the best profession on earth. That what you're about to enter into and do is the most important thing in your life. That you're going to go to a job and you're going to give 100% from Day One.

That you're going to continue to learn every day on that job, and that you're going to begin very quickly to form opinions, and that you're going to have the guts to share them within the structure of the organization that you're working in and to perform at your highest level, and you're going to look for every opportunity to do so.

You're going to take every opportunity (no one gives you opportunities—you have to take them) to learn and to grow.

You're going to understand the community in which you work, whether it's academic, public, or school library. You're going to know who leads it and who follows. You're going to associate yourself with leaders. You're going to learn from them; you're going to observe them, and you're going to choose which for you are the good ones and which are the bad ones, and then you're going to overlay those observations into your own skills.

You're going to decide early on, within the first five years of your professional life, what role you want to play in the profession.

Then you also need to know when to move. I never wanted to leave a job because I didn't like it. I've looked at opportunities that were something I wanted to go to, rather than away from. And I'll often counsel staff who are really upset or disgruntled: go to something, don't leave something. You watch, and the people whose careers seem to spiral downward—they are running from something.

There are some incredible opportunities in this profession. I am not one of those who say we are dying or dead.

STEPANIAN: You have to have some kind of networking. You have to develop networking among your peers. It takes a lot of time, it does not come overnight. It could take five, six, seven years for some of that to develop.

Part of it is by contacts through associations and being involved in a state and a national association. There has been many a committee that I've been on that has not accomplished very much, but that lets me go away from a meeting knowing that I've made contact with somebody and that has been so valuable.

You can't stay by yourself. You can't be holed up in a room by yourself. You have to constantly explore any avenue that you possibly can. People sometimes wonder why I in a school library get involved with public libraries and academic libraries and special libraries that in Cleveland basically are business libraries, but the reason is simple: Those other people and places expand my contacts.

Right now there's no one else in my district who can understand all the problems I face. But a group of us in the Cleveland area have lunch maybe once every eight weeks, just trying to share concerns, commonalities, and whatever else may come up. Sometimes, just by one statement, you learn a great deal from another person.

CHISHOLM: I am convinced that leaders develop. Leaders with potential and innate capabilities have to develop skills in public speaking, in written communication, in being analytical, in being able to work with groups, and in being able to build consensus.

And they must be able to make decisions. A leader must gather information and gather facts, but eventually the leader gets to a point where the decision must be made. In an ideal situation one might say, "Well, I would like to have more information," or "I would like to wait until certain conditions occur." But a leader must accept the fact that he or she has the best information available and then must make a decision.

Being able to make decisions in a timely fashion based on good, sound judgment is a skill that comes through experience.

Young leaders can begin by working in their state organizations and their state chapters. They can demonstrate willingness to take on responsibilities. In their local libraries, they can assume increasing responsibility and develop leadership skills.

Activity in ALA can help provide learning opportunities, such as work in committees, serving as a committee chair, making reports, taking on research assignments, working in groups, chairing meetings, participating in council meetings or working on various activities of a division, a chapter, or a round table.

FARBER: My first advice is to follow someone in his or her position who wasn't doing a very good job so you immediately have credibility. But after that, understand the environment. That's very important.

In a college situation it means understanding the politics of the institution, the purpose of the institution, the personnel of the institution, to know it well, to know its history.

It also means in any academic situation to understand and appreciate and to want to promote the purposes of higher education. To keep in mind that the library is not an end in itself. The library is serving the purposes of whatever institution it is connected with.

DUMONT: Young librarians need to make sure they feel comfortable with the specialization they want to do. It need not always be what they consider glamorous. They need to look at their strengths and allow themselves to specialize where their strengths are.

Young librarians who come to me to work have to show me that they really want to do that, and that they really want to continue to learn and grow. Not just be a librarian, get a paycheck, and go home. Rather, they want to continue to grow and be innovative. They're willing to come to me and say, "I think we can do things another way; what would you think?" I look for people who want to do that, who want to be able to grow and not become stagnant in their profession.

My advice is find something that you're interested in and see if there's a need. Perhaps it's in technology. Perhaps it's becoming a specialist in CD-ROM or in artificial intelligence or in something that's going to come up in the future. And really work on that emphasis.

Or if you want to be a public service librarian, how can you apply these technologies to the public service area? How can you help foster the future growth of the institution and the library, the learning resources center?

We in community colleges do a lot of educational development. You may want to work as an educational developer, helping faculty develop better resources and techniques, or making them aware of what's available to help them teach. That's extremely important.

You might want to become involved in a community college production of telecourses. We at Dallas are the largest producer of telecourses in the country. Perhaps that's another specialty you can get involved with.

The nonprint area. The media resource area. The development of computer interaction. We have a lot of computer labs we are responsible for. We are looking for more and more computer-oriented professionals.

We're developing interactions of learning with computing resources, learning labs, and skills labs. Those are the people who will get the jobs in the future, and the skills that are needed.

COOPER: You go to the state conferences and the national conferences. You go to all the local and state workshops.

There's one thing about some folks that I just don't understand. How can you be a librarian and not belong to ALA and get all the publications in your field? Everyone who's a librarian should belong. And you have to participate in the workshops. There's no question about it. Library school doesn't teach you all there is to know about being a librarian.

ASP: As operations of librarians become more and more complicated, it's just not possible for people to hold all the information in their heads anymore, so they have to delegate more, and they have to spend more time developing staff. A person coming right out of library school can expect to start learning some leadership skills on the job from the first day.

Leadership is developing people. It's articulating visions, it's building consensus, working with other people to build consensus, identifying a future that everybody buys into and can move toward together. You can do that in virtually any job and at virtually any level.

By the time people have gone to library school and gotten degrees, they are in most cases going to be supervising other people. They're going to have to start building those visions, working with other people building consensus, identifying direction and making sure the people under them have the tools they need to get the whole organization in that direction.

HEIM: We give students a lot of opportunity to do leading for student associations.

I tell them at the orientation at the beginning of their time with us that these activities, this identification of leadership roles within the school, are the kinds of roles that I hope they take when they graduate. So we try to develop in our students at the beginning of their studies an interest in a leadership position in a student committee or service on a faculty committee.

If they want to change the world, as I hope they do, they need to know they can do this best from positions of leadership. A commitment to greater things than self is requisite to change the status quo.

VASILAKIS: Get a job with a library that has a good leader in it already, and watch what happens. Just model yourself after that person. That's what I did.

WHITNEY: Become involved. Begin to work at the committee level, to get involved in issues being discussed by the professionals. Make your views known.

You have to be willing to take a chance because people may disagree with you along the way. You learn a lot by getting out there and getting involved.

There are a lot of politics involved, too.

Rising to a leadership position in a school library means that people respect you. You have to be able to communicate well with others; if you are knowledgeable but can't communicate, you're not likely to be successful.

In a school, rising to a leadership position means that you have to have gathered along the way administrative ability. Without administrative ability, you're not going to be put in leadership positions. It's important within a school to serve on committees that really have a chance to make a change. Without the background in administration, you aren't likely to be in that position.

And all this isn't likely to change in the near future. Ten years from now, you'll still have to be knowledgeable, you'll have to be able to communicate. All of that places a heavy responsibility on the school librarians in the future because we constantly will have to be updated. The field is changing so rapidly, and the only way to keep up is by immersing yourself in the literature and by continuing education.

BERGER: First of all, going to library school is not enough. You need to work at the nuts and bolts for a while. If, for example, you want to manage a science library someday, you better understand what it means to develop a scientific collection. What are the parameters for resources development? And you'd better understand what is required of a reference person dealing with a particular population.

The best advice I can give is determine what kind of library interests you. Then learn as much as you possibly can about its users and what will be required to serve those users well. And third, find a library in which you can, early on, be given programmatic responsibilities and do them well. Then see what happens.

MASON: Someone who wants to be a leader probably has already taken the first step themselves. Working closely with leaders is useful. I would try to apprentice myself to someone I admired. I would try to get a job that would allow me to see how that person functioned.

There are a number of places in the library field that have formalized programs for doing that, which place someone who is young and ambitious and talented with an experienced administrator, leader. That is an important kind of matching up.

One thing I did when I was much younger that turned out to have a very important impact on me was I wrote an article called "Five Women," and I interviewed five women who were leaders in this profession. It was a very special experience for me to sit and talk with them and ask them questions—all kinds of prying questions—for several hours and then try to make sense of it. I think I probably got more out of that exercise than anybody who read the article later.

SUMMERS: Get into professional organizations. Don't just be a member, be a participant. Identify the kinds of committees that you're interested in, go to their meetings and present yourself as being interested and able.

If the organization you're dealing with, like ALA, is large enough to have specialized professional staff, identify yourself to those folks early on, and say, "I'm interested; I'm willing to work; I'll carry my share of the load."

In any organization or any field, you have to go through a period of paying your dues, where you do some of the scut kind of work so you get to take on greater responsibilities. You just have to accept that. You're not going to start out as chair of the committee. You're probably going to have to do some other kinds of things.

You have to do some self-analysis and say, if I want to be in a leadership position, what does it take and what kinds of skill building do I need to do?

For example, early on I realized I needed to strengthen my ability in public speaking. So I spent an apprenticeship of four or five years in an organization called Toastmasters. That was extremely valuable to me. I got reinforcement and training and experiences of a low-level, low-threat kind of nature that I could never have gotten otherwise, and I've reaped benefits from that.

You have to be willing to be fairly self-critical. You have to find somebody who when you get up and speak will say, "Bill, that was good . . . except." That's one thing Toastmasters gives you, but you have to get it from other people in the field, too.

And you have to develop people who think well of you and who will sort of sponsor you into things.

WEDGEWORTH: I try to urge students to choose their first job very carefully. To choose the first job, not only in terms of whom they're going to be working with, what kind of job, but also whether this is going to be a learning experience upon which they can build, whether it's a very technical first job or a very general first job. They want to be sure they can learn something in the first two or three years.

And then, always choose your jobs very carefully. Look at the people you're going to be working with. Look at the organization. Make sure that this adds to your complement of experience and is going to give you something that you find valuable.

All too frequently a big mistake is that people choose jobs that they really shouldn't choose, for reasons that are extraneous to the position itself.

It's too easy to pick a job because you like to live in a given place. And then you'll find you like the place but you're miserable on the job. On the job is where you spend most of your time. You can't enjoy a place if you're miserable on the job.

Choosing jobs where there are people, either in a managerial position or in the leadership position, they respect and admire, and having an opportunity to see how they operate within their organization is vital.

McDONALD: Choose very carefully where you work. You need to be in a place where you will get opportunities to learn, where they are doing exciting things, where there are very bright people.

If a beginner can get into an area that is innovative, and dynamic, and changing, and is allowed to expand, that's the road to follow.

Investigate whether a job will allow time and money for professional conferences and workshops.

Pick your boss and pick your environment. Look at where the library is placed in the organization, no matter what kind of library it is. Do you report to the personnel office or do you report ⬍ to the vice-president for research? Take a good look at that. It may not get you any more money, but it's going to give you a different perspective and allow you to grow professionally.

GORAL: Pick out someone you admire in the field, and say, I want to be like this person, or I like this person's style. Or pick a few individuals and say, I like this style, they do this really well. And really sort of follow along and, in essence, have that person or those persons as your mentor.

It doesn't necessarily have to be a very close relationship. You can follow what library leaders are doing just by reading the literature and being aware of what they're up to in the library field.

DOUGHERTY: I'd look for a library where there's a sense of excitement, a library which has a reputation for helping young staff to develop, a library that is most likely to stretch your ability and will allow young staff to make mistakes and take risks. There are a few of those libraries around but not too many.

EASTMAN: Your most important decision is going to be your choice of your first boss. While they're interviewing you, you'd better be interviewing them. Don't go into a "closed corporation," into a library that has not moved toward the twenty-first century. Take a job where you'll find a mentor, or many mentors, and people who really want to make changes and have the courage to stick together to get the changes made. Look for a library with a sense of community or unity of purpose, a place where people are interested in their work and dedicated to doing it well in concert with others with whom they interact.

And read Mary Gaver's new book, *A Braided Cord: Memoirs of a School Librarian* (The Scarecrow Press, 1988). It tells great lessons on how leaders are made.

SMITH: The older I get the more I think it's just a bunch of circumstances that come together and work all at once.

Beginners can identify people that have been there, or who are there, and they can observe and hope. But I know a lot of people don't learn from observation, they learn from experience.

I don't know that you can guarantee anybody that he or she can be a leader. I've seen too many good people, competent good people, well educated, bright, who are not leaders at all. Never will be, because they're not strong and confident inside and then they don't have the desire, either, to expose themselves.

Most people want a comfortable existence. And it's not comfortable when you're out there on the front line. You're the first one who's going to be shot at. Most people don't want that.

Some of us, given the choice, might not have wanted that, either. Circumstances and then the sense of responsibility just made us get out in front.

How can the library associations encourage more leadership development?

CHISHOLM: I would like ALA to be able to identify 50 young people entering the profession. Ideally they would have been in the profession three or four years so that they have some professional background and have identified the direction they wish to go.

These are not just people who want to become directors of public libraries, but they all have strong capabilities in some special area.

I would like to have them be able to attend some formal classes so that they would participate in formal instruction on the definitions of leadership and study the skills that are required in leadership. They would study the different leadership styles so that they would have a formal foundation on which to base their future learning. The best way to develop these specialized skills would be to identify a number of more mature professionals who have really accomplished a lot in the areas to which the younger professionals aspire. The young people would associate with the veterans and learn leadership skills through direct contact.

I don't mean just mentoring; this is bigger and broader than mentoring. I would expect them to observe, participate, practice, and then be able to move out and attempt many things on their own. If we could add a complement of 50 each year, by 1998 we would have 500 young leaders who had gone through this experiential track, and by then the first ones would have gained another 10 years experience in the profession. Then we would have a core of very strong leaders.

The psychological aspect of repeating the message that we need leaders, that we need persons with strong capabilities, will have almost as much impact as the actual experiences. We have spent many years convincing everyone that we're meek, mild, service-oriented, and that nothing beyond those characteristics is needed. Now we must spend equal time saying we need persons who are risk-takers, who are convincing, who are able and eager to move out and make a strong statement in support of libraries. It will take a long time to accomplish this, but the 500 will have a powerful influence.

If we're going to do this right, then these young leaders will need some released time from their regular jobs, three or four weeks every six months. This must be funded if the plan is to be implemented in an ideal, optimum way.

BERGER: One of the first things which has to be addressed is the agenda for the next White House conference. The Association and the profession have to be better prepared to articulate what we expect to accomplish in the next century and what we expect our role to be.

Finally, we're giving a little attention to a national preservation program. What is the point of talking about library service in the twenty-first century if there's nothing left to read because it's all crumbling and rotting? I am very concerned about our lack of attention to this very important problem.

There are ways in which ALA could not only highlight some of the problems in this area but publicize the efforts, for example, of publishers to combat the problems. Every publisher who voluntarily agrees to use permanent paper should receive public accolades for doing so.

One of the things that bothers me most about the profession is that we don't do a thing about honoring our own, or honoring those people who have helped us. We have to improve our corporate memory. We've got to get back to the nuts and bolts of what it is we're going to take into the new century and in what condition. And how we're going to serve people. I'm speaking broadly now for the whole profession, not just for special librarians.

We could not have dissuaded the Reagan Administration from the dollar devaluation policy, but the large research libraries and libraries like my own would have been much better prepared had we foreseen what was happening and had begun to prepare for it. Again, we reacted to something which hit us right between the eyes.

The new tax law may do that to us this year. There again, we're not too well prepared either at the national level or at the local level to cope. When librarians realize they can no longer deduct their dues from their income taxes, you're apt to see a lot more selectivity about memberships. I think that could have monumental impact on some of the associations.

COOPER: You wouldn't have any parks or land saved for the benefit of everyone if you didn't have environmentalists, and you won't have libraries unless you have advocates. Advocates are essential in this highly competitive world. If you do not have advocates for libraries, professional librarians simply cannot get all they need from funding bodies.

The role of ALTA is to educate the trustees to carry out their role more properly and adequately and to educate librarians to make use of volunteers, of advocates.

You learn as a trustee. You don't come to meetings in order to tell a librarian what to do. You come to learn about the library and its operation and to give a user's view or a businessperson's view of how the service can be improved.

Trustees ought to expect of the library the same good management and service to the user that a business has to give if it is to remain productive. They ought to encourage the librarian and the library staff to participate in all of the things that will enlarge their view so that they can continue their growth as individuals helping to serve the public.

WEDGEWORTH: What any organization like that can do is to have ways of systematically identifying individuals who have great potential for leadership and then putting those persons in a position to really understand how the field is organized and where the field is likely to go and what role they may be able to play, so that they choose their direction more effectively.

We don't have a really coherent view of the field right now because there's been so much fragmentation and so much rapid movement driven by technology and economics.

For example, I could say that there are really only three basic professional specialties in our field. There's the specialty that deals with information systems, including bibliographic systems. We've got resources and information service, putting groups of people that you can describe together with the kinds of materials that they really need for their work. The third specialty is management, putting those systems and services together in some form that meets the parameters of the given institution. All the technical specialties that we have will fit into one, and sometimes more than one, of those three groupings.

And then if you talk about the environments in which we operate, we really only have three basic environments. You've got the environment of the public agency, whether it's at the international, federal, state, or local level. You've got the environment of education, whether it's higher education or secondary education or elementary education, whether it's public or private. The third environment is the private sector.

And if you look at it that way and we get our people to focus their attention precisely on how they prepare themselves for careers that relate those professional specialties to the environment in which we operate, I think that we identify the people and set them on a course by narrowing the view of what is truly definitive about the opportunities in our field, rather than having people so early identify such narrow specialties.

The preparation for narrow specialties is important, but they've got to be able to see a broader framework within which those specialties are practiced. Associations do a very good job of that through the way they group their members. That tends to keep the very narrow specializations from capturing so many people.

EASTMAN: Sustain and strengthen continuing education efforts in every area. ALA does a lot to teach people what they don't find out at home. Those ground down in positions at home and not allowed to use or develop leadership capabilities can do these things in ALA, SLA, state library associations, management groups, formal courses, and other networking groups.

Obviously, the ALA staff are leaders. So there's a lot of access to leadership in ALA if that's what you're looking for.

Of course, one doesn't get up on Wednesday and say, "Today I'll be a leader." As I meet younger people in LAMA, I try to reveal the way I think about answering a question, or how I approach a certain kind of topic or piece of work in the division.

What we seem not to be doing, not just in libraries, but in lots of other areas in this world, is developing or using our abilities to make connections. The linkages among things—the if-this-then-that, causes and effects, actions and reactions—aren't being pursued or discovered or analyzed as much as they need to be. Our intellectual lives are fragmenting and segmenting. These synapses aren't occurring as often as they need to.

What new skills and attributes must the leader have by 1998?

GORAL: Library administrators, library leaders, have to become much more astute as far as politics are concerned. They need to become better fiscal managers. They need to communicate to people that what we do is good and what we do is necessary, and we're just as important as any other organization they deal with.

Libraries and library leadership have taken a back seat; they really haven't been vocal about how important they are. That's slowly beginning to change now as we get more vocal about it.

COOPER: More of them ought to develop a little charisma. And their skills must be technological, political, managerial.

As a trustee, I think the most important skill is the ability to motivate and deal with library professionals and with any type of person outside the library, whether it's a volunteer or a politician, to help get their programs funded and to help them grow.

CHISHOLM: Very strong, capable, self-confident persons who will speak up for their profession.

If that means going to Congress to testify for adequate funding, they should be able to. If it means speaking to their state legislators, they should do it. They must be able to make strong, convincing statements to their local boards, whether it's the school board or the board of trustees of public libraries. They must be able to speak to the members of the city council. We're far past the time when a library can meet its optimum commitment and goals with personnel who are submissive and accepting.

Librarians must take strong initiatives, be convincing in their presentations, be competent in analyzing numbers and financial budgets, and make convincing presentations to the persons responsible for funding. They must also speak up on issues as important to us as intellectual freedom. We must be very strong in fighting censorship.

We must be assertive in implementing opportunities for equal access for all people. With technology, there is the possibility of a wide gap between those who will have access to information and those who may not be able to pay to have access to information. Librarians must take strong initiatives to be certain that this inequity of access does not develop into a debilitating gap between the "haves" and "have-nots."

Librarians must be proactive, they must move out, they must create an image that is different from the submissive, total service-oriented aspect. The future of the profession depends on this kind of leadership.

The ALA theme for 1988 was leadership. Why is the library field so late to concentrate on this important subject?

HEIM: Librarians have worked really hard to develop the resources to give to people. We tend to think very hard in terms of what we can provide to the users. So much so that we haven't perhaps realized—we've realized it but is hasn't been articulated until this year by Margaret Chisholm—that the only way to get those resources to people is to have leaders who can go out and get the resources.

Unfortunately in this country you can't just sit here with a good library and expect that good things will come to it. For a long time, many librarians felt that our product was so good we didn't need to sell it. And now I think it's clear that we need leaders who will make sure that the word gets out and make sure that we have the resources.

CHISHOLM: Because the principles on which librarianship were founded all focused on service and because librarianship started as a feminine profession. Virtually all the early librarians were women, and they were imbued with the idea of nurturing and caring.

Even now, at least a third of the students we have coming into the profession really come with that kind of an expectation and intent. So strongly do they feel this idea of service and embody this concept, that even when we have required courses in management and administration, about a third of them say they do not want to have anything to do with management or administration. They say, "I am here to serve the public. I want to work with people. I love books. I want to be of help to provide information."

I do not believe that attitude is wrong, as I think it's a very important and humane part of the profession, and I think that accounts for much of the success of the profession. But at the same time, I am convinced that if the profession is going to move ahead financially and become a strength and a power in the future, it has to have a different kind of philosophy on the part of its professionals.

SUMMERS: Because it took us a long time to put a label on the need. We tend to be oriented to the technical side of the discipline, and so it took a need to say at this time we need to develop leaders. We need to look at what our processes are for identifying and developing leaders.

That's not to say we haven't had some really strong leaders over the years. ALA is the kind of effective organization that it is because of its people. We've just never set out to systematically say can we structure processes to produce leaders.

COOPER: ALA has been going through a very wearying revolution—the planning process. First came the leadership seminar. That was when the seed was planted out of which has come all the rest. Then came the planning process, and it's absolutely the most incredible amount of work and gobbledygook.

The result is going to be that the people coming up through the divisions, through the planning processes, are going to be leaders and they're going to be vocal.

If there had been more funding for the top-notch professionals to spend time between meetings doing this enormous amount of work and study and research, you could have gotten it done more rapidly. But these people were trying to earn a living as well as do the association's work.

WEDGEWORTH: The choice of the major theme for an ALA conference is really the choice of the president. And there are so many different possible themes that there's no simple explanation as to why it took so long.

We've talked about leadership in different ways. For example, back in 1982 in Los Angeles, Carol Nemeyer's theme was "Connections." Well, she wasn't talking about connections in the abstract, she was talking about connections that build toward leadership.

We've had a number of different themes that can be related to leadership, but no one has really focused specifically on leadership itself. That's a very difficult theme around which to build a program because it's so abstract and you have to have a specific idea that you want to put into effect in choosing a theme like that.

BERGER: That's not peculiar to ALA. It's true of all library and information associations. I think it's because librarians have been taught, and many of them believe, that their role is to serve, not to lead. I don't think that's true; I've never thought it was true. Unfortunately, a lot of librarians are simply not comfortable in a leadership role.

Where did you get the idea for the leadership theme for ALA?

CHISHOLM: I read everything that had to do with mission and goal statements of the American Library Association. I read all documents relating to the ALA strategic long-range plan. I thought through every statement I could find on the goals of the profession, the challenges to the professional organizations, and I tried to think in what I would call a cycle, the cause and effect. I tried to analyze what would be the underlying solutions and determine what would help us achieve our stated goals.

Inevitably, no matter how I did the analysis, or at what point in the cycle I started or ended, it all came back to people and the accomplishments of the professionals. The accomplishments in the profession all seemed to point to individuals who had the capabilities, the ingenuity, and the drive to provide that leadership.

What could library educators and managers do to increase innovation and entrepreneurship within the library field?

CHISHOLM: Get as much funding as possible. It usually takes dollars to be innovative; it takes dollars to fund creative research. In addition, you've got to provide research time and equipment.

You have to have supportive management to allow the creator or the innovator to function in an ambience that is stimulating and encouraging.

WEDGEWORTH: Opportunity is going to play a great role in that.

If our students come out of our graduate education program understanding that everything that happens at an institution will not be handed to them in the form of the annual budget, that there are certain kinds of things that have to be created and certain opportunities that present certain possibilities, they can be entrepreneurial and innovative.

Awareness is probably the key element. They have to be aware that there is a responsibility to do those kinds of things and then be alert to the opportunities. That's about as much as the graduate schools can do in preparing students, along with making them aware of specific activities that demonstrate our thinking.

Out in the field, it's going to be difficult, because we still have a very strong orientation toward having the governmental authority that supervises the institution, or the parent organization that provides for the library information service.

Strong orientation is already there and you have to fight against that a little bit in order to promote entrepreneurial behavior. At the same time, you don't want students to ignore the responsibilities of those sponsoring authorities. They can't expect to cut your support by 40% and have you go out and find that difference. They're not living up to their responsibilities in that regard.

So we're in a delicate position in terms of promoting entrepreneurial behavior. Even though we know we want budgets to grow in the near term at a faster rate than they will normally be supported, there has to be some initiative and creativity injected into the system.

COOPER: There are leaders I see at ALA emerging right now who are promoting it. I don't think anyone is solving the problem for the smaller library or the small institution and the only solution may be that as younger people step into the library profession, they'll be more experienced in marketing and they'll just naturally assume the role that we see the leaders doing now.

Chapter 11

Libraries in Society

This is the first of three "combination" chapters, each about a variety of topics. Included here are comments about whether libraries today mean as much as they used to, libraries and solving illiteracy, the information poor and their loss of access, and the importance of PR to a library.

———— ♦ ♦ ♦ ————

The significance of libraries in society—do they mean as much now as they used to?

SMITH: No matter what we do technologically, or what we do with the information age, or what we do with the information specialist, some institution needs to value what things mean. I don't find any institution other than the library that has historically or traditionally had an interest in ideas, knowledge.

Libraries are the only public institutions that provide a means to look at what knowledge is all about. And what it means to us. All points of view for all people, all ages. We're the only ones. And I don't want to see that sacrificed with an overemphasis on the how, the how we do it. The important thing is that we do it and know why.

What do things mean to our society? I want kids to think about that, not just play with a computer and extract facts. I want them to think about "Where do I fit in this world now that it's so small, and I can tap into any corner of it?"

A library is a sense of place where you can find out who you are in the broadest sense and who others are in the more specific sense. You can learn about those subjects that we don't talk about, that they don't teach in school, that you might get in a religious setting but in a slanted way.

We can learn how to invest in Southeast Asia, the Pacific Rim. We can learn how to speak the languages. We can learn about the cultures. We can learn what the people like, and what they eat, and where they live and such, but the library is probably the only place that you can go and find out, who are they? Beyond what they eat. Who are they and what are their beliefs, and what made them that way and what is their history? That's what we can find out in a library that no other institution can give you.

COOPER: To the newly developing communities, the library is the major cultural center. In time, in my county, they add a museum and perhaps a performing arts center, but the library is really the basic cultural center for every community until they can add all the gingerbread.

In an old city up North a library might get lost in the cultural picture, but in a developing state, the library is just about the first public good and public culture that is provided.

Generally, it's first provided free by a few people getting together and saying, let's have a library. As it grows, it's usually the citizens who keep working to build a building and when you finally have the brick and mortar, that becomes your cultural center.

In Florida, it is my impression that as we have grown, our libraries have become really very much stronger and have a greater role in the community.

On the other hand, we have many people who really pay no attention to the library at all. There's just a whole culture out there that is totally separated from libraries, from youth on. I hope that group doesn't get overwhelming and that the current interest in literacy/illiteracy will maybe get the pendulum moving back.

What libraries are going to mean in 1998 to society as a whole depends on the people who are now working for libraries. It depends on volunteers and the librarians. If the librarians are able to develop the concept of providing information, if they're able to create libraries that are absolutely essential to people's development and people's employment, then they're going to be very important places. If they just remain passive and they're not out front and they're not mixing in the marketing arena and the political arena, then they're going to die on the vine.

The difference will be whether the library staff members are aggressive in providing information, service to people, and are very up-to-date and modern in their relationship with all the political bodies. And if they are able to mobilize dedicated volunteers.

WISENER: Libraries definitely mean as much now as they used to. With the innovative ideas that have come forth with the new technology, we're reaching people who used to be in the non-user class. I'm hoping that is where growth is going to come from. The technology helps reach people who weren't using the library before.

For example, we're trying to supply material for farmers. I don't think we had that many farmers coming in until we had a federal grant that built our program. Now we have a lot more.

We bought books and materials for what farmers requested. We have magazines that we previously had not had. Since there are all of these things now in the line of adult education, we're bringing in people who are illiterate and are seeking help in that area.

We have computers for them to work with and on. It's the most exciting thing just to watch them and see the thrill as they learn to use that computer.

Of course, we're far away from the little quiet library that I went to as a youngster and tried to read through the stacks. The people in the library field are now more innovative. The library didn't used to be known as an area of great innovation. It was the hush-hush, quiet-quiet, little-bun-on-the-back-of-the-head place.

All the depth of literature, the feeling when you walk into a library, the smell of a library, a frequent user has to know just what the odor is and what a delight it is. And the quality of life that it offers the community.

It's like any cultural institution. I think it puts a definite quality into a community. You can't put your finger on that and it's a trite expression to keep talking about the quality of life, but there it is. There's a part of the feeling that's important for human growth, community growth. It adds to a healthy community, a word symphony type of offering to the community, but more than that. After all we've all gone into pictures and we've gone into tapes, and we've gone into other things, so it isn't entirely words. It covers all cultural things now.

WEDGEWORTH: We spend a lot of time talking to ourselves about the structure and the complexity and the significance of libraries and information systems. But we don't spend enough time articulating to the public what our objectives are in serving their needs and interests and how these systems that we are developing will pay off in terms of improved services to them in the future.

We haven't articulated our objectives so that they relate closely enough to local, state, and national priorities. Because if we're
going to be successful in competing for scarce funds—and the
funds are going to be even more scarce in the future—we've got to
be sure that we contribute to things that the tax-paying population
or the corporate officers feel are important.

This means public libraries have to show that there are im-
pressive resources that libraries can bring to bear on addressing
the literacy problems. They've got to show that they can be an
important adjunct to small businesses that can't afford their own
information departments and can't afford their own libraries. For
academic libraries, we've got to demonstrate that libraries and the
kind of self-teaching information services that we are familiar with
can be important components of teaching and research and learning at colleges and universities.

Then we can indeed support faculties in ways that they probably haven't considered in the past. Not in terms of teaching the
content of their subject, but we know things about the structures
of literatures, the different kinds of formats of information, that
the average faculty member simply doesn't understand even in his
or her own discipline.

We've got to find a way to add that to the arsenal of knowledge and methodological skills that we expect each student to
emerge from the college or university with, so that they in a sense
become independent learners and learn not only a certain amount
of content, but also techniques and how to assess, how to go about
problem solving in an information world in ways that we don't
presently teach them.

Illiteracy. Schools haven't been able to solve it. Will libraries?

De GENNARO: Libraries have a role to play, an important role,
but I don't think that they're going to solve the whole literacy
problem. I think libraries can tackle only a certain part of it.

The reason is that it's not just a literacy problem; it's a
problem of poverty, and it's not a question of teaching people to
read; it's really a question of helping the poor and the
disadvantaged to raise their standard of living.

It's really a very serious social problem of poverty and alien-
ation. You can't simply teach people to read. You have to raise
them up and do a lot of other things for them—find them jobs,

give them a certain kind of security—before they're ready to learn to read.

I would characterize the literacy problem as a continuum, and over on the left are people living at the fringe of society, people who are hungry, ill-housed, and unemployed. All the way over to the right are people who are functioning members of society but who for one reason or another didn't learn to read, but now are ready to learn to read, and I think that's the group the library can reach. These are people who at least have it together enough to come to the library and to take advantage of the services that we offer to them.

But the biggest percentage, three-quarters of them, we will never see because they're really not ready for the kinds of services that the library can provide.

How those 75% are going to be taken care of is a national problem. It's the problem of the homeless, the problem of the poor, the problem of the unemployed, the problem of that part of our society that is being bypassed and left aside. And all of the predictions and forecasts that I've seen are that the problem is going to become increasingly serious as we move toward the year 2000.

You bring up the notion of information rich and information poor. If I'm in the bypassed part of society, I really am not going to have as much access, am I?

De GENNARO: That's right. The role of the public library here as we come to the end of the twentieth century and go on into the twenty-first, is the same as it was when libraries like these were formed at the end of the nineteenth century. Their role was to make books and other reading materials available to people who at that time were information poor, print poor.

Now as we enter an information society where information is in electronic form, the role of the public library is reaffirmed. It is to provide information in electronic as well as in print form to the information poor. The way we meet that demand and the form that the information is in may be changing, but the basic function is still there.

There is a need for the public libraries to make this information, increasingly in electronic form, available to the information poor. That's really a reaffirmation of our function, so I don't buy the idea that the information technology is making the public library obsolete. On the contrary, information technology is reaffirming the role of the public library as we enter the next century.

MASON: The illiteracy problem is one that is larger than libraries can solve. The appropriate thing for libraries to do is to work with other community groups in a cohesive manner so that programs and services are mutually supportive.

In Cleveland, we provide materials for adults who are beginning to read or learning to read. We work with the literacy groups, the literacy training groups, to make those available to people so that they are aware that the materials are available at the library. Very often beginning readers will be brought to the library and shown where the materials are and introduced to them in that way. We provide space for tutoring programs.

Libraries are still very positive forces in communities, far more than schools, for instance. It's exciting to see libraries maintain that positive position in the communities. And so as a place for a tutoring program, it's a very good one. People aren't ashamed to be seen going to a library. We can provide space, we can provide materials, and then we can work with the actual tutoring groups to extend awareness throughout the community.

What's the importance of PR to a library?

EASTMAN: Put to the test, a lot of library directors indicate that PR and fundraising are "soft" areas, not real library functions. In the years ahead they may pay quite a price for that attitude.

PR has long been treated by many library directors as a nice thing to do when they "get around to it," or something to do just before a bond issue, or just before a budget hearing or whatever. They will even take the time to reach out into the community, have a reception, get out a brochure, gather a few facts.

Any major academic, public, or school library today that isn't planning to undertake a continuing fundraising program is being very short-sighted. There is money out there and people do care about libraries. They may not know what DIALOG is, or VTLS, or NOTIS—or care. The one thing that libraries have that still draws emotional response from people—and money out of their pockets—is books.

And there's nothing wrong with using books to promote a library, so long as the gifts that come in can be spent to a large degree in an unrestricted fashion across the board for the items and services most needed. As a general promotional vehicle for libraries, there is nothing better at the moment than the book.

PR should not be a half-time job for somebody in larger libraries. It should not be a sometime thing. It should be a sustained, building, professional program. The absence of that kind of library public relations in all kinds of libraries is one reason that libraries and librarians are so invisible.

I'm not talking about running around patting yourself on the back. I'm talking about a conscientious effort to capture what it is in the library experience that contributes uniquely to a person's life and packaging that, telling the outside world about it, and telling the outside world to come to get it. And making them want to come to get it.

That kind of gutsy relations, ongoing and sustained, will lead to successful fundraising ventures and more, including realistic budgets that are supported continually by the appropriate individuals and groups.

Chapter 12

Commercial Competition

This "combination chapter" is about commercial competition in providing information, how libraries and publishers relate, the special problems of special libraries, and resource sharing.

——— ♦ ♦ ♦ ———

Do you see the libraries getting a lot more commercial competition in providing information?

ASP: It's going to be the private sector relating to libraries and selling information to libraries, rather than necessarily selling information to individuals.

Some folks who have tried to market information directly to the individual have been really disappointed because the market hasn't been there. Sometimes people don't identify their need as an information need either, so they wouldn't necessarily turn to a broker or seller of information.

While there are commercial firms that are increasingly selling computer-based information services, their market is the library, and it's the library then that makes those things available to the user. Libraries are going to have to decide whether they can secure the funding to support those costs or are going to have to pass some of those costs on to the user.

STRONG: There are certain elements in society that have always been "competition"—book stores and video shops and television. If television isn't our most incredible competitor, I don't know what is. And libraries are their own worst competitors.

Before we blame the commercial sector, we'd better take a hard look at ourselves first. On the other hand, yes, there is an incredibly growing commercialization of information. Look in the government arena alone. We're having to buy more and more of it back.

I sat on the Lacy Access Commission, and I saw us argue more among ourselves as to whether what we are going to put out would meet ALA policy. Well, who cares? Certainly, I don't know of any government official or governor who cares whether freedom of access meets ALA's policy.

I look at resource sharing and the payment to nonpublic libraries for sharing information as an economic development issue, not as a library issue. And when I talk to the legislators, it's on those terms. It's not in terms of the need to be supportive of DIALOG and SDC and Lockheed, SRI and Rand Corporation.

We pay Rand Corporation for interlibrary loans they make to public libraries because that's economic development support of the state's economy. And if we're going to keep the research coming in, the libraries have got to say we're part of economic development.

A lot of librarians are extremely uncomfortable with that. But we've got to be in there with AT&T, Pacific Telesis, which is now the wholly owned company in California of AT&T, as they develop new information products and make sure that libraries keep their role in disseminating information for the public good, the broad good of the state, of the citizens.

With the California Library Association, we successfully fought through the Public Utilities Commission Pacific Bell's decision to stop providing telephone directories to libraries. And PUC came down on our side and said as a matter of public policy, Pacific Bell will spend that million dollars and provide that information.

So competition? Yeah. It's always been there. I think it's going to get more intense. I am worried that there's too much competition within the libraries, with the publicly funded libraries, as there is with the commercial sector. Too often we structure that discussion as being us against them. It's more often us against us.

The relationship between librarians and libraries and publishers. How do you see that getting along?

GORAL: Sometimes in an adversary position because publishers are beginning to publish materials on recorded format.

I'm wondering if in the next 10 years whether publishers will say, no, we're not going to be able to give you the copyright permission for this, or, we've recorded this material and therefore it's for sale to anyone who's interested. In that sense I see it as an adversary relationship.

In another sense I see us working with publishers very closely because we are probably going to be recording more information for the blind and handicapped and we're going to need that permission.

We're going to have to come to an understanding that, yes, materials can and will be available on recorded format for the general public, but we also need special permission for our own recording.

Do libraries for the blind and physically handicapped have special problems that other libraries don't have?

GORAL: We're in essence a warehousing facility. We provide library service, but we don't provide it in the same sense that a public library does.

Libraries for the blind and physically handicapped in the United States need to look at themselves as libraries, rather than as book warehousing facilities. We need to communicate to the people who matter, the people with the money, that we are not a warehouse, we are a library.

We need better locations. Libraries for the blind and physically handicapped traditionally have been put in places that you wouldn't ordinarily find a public library. For instance, in a basement of a building. And sometimes inaccessible places off a viaduct or off a freeway, which makes it difficult or impossible for the person who is unable to use a traditional car to get in to use the service.

Does a corporate library have a problem in sharing with other libraries?

BERGER: Yes. It depends on a corporate library's management and there are certainly some corporations out there which do not encourage cooperation with those they perceive to be their competitors. In addition, many special libraries, ours included, handle proprietary data.

The Bureau makes its facilities available to private industry for proprietary research. If we have a laboratory which is not duplicated anywhere else in the world, for example, we will permit private firms to come in and do research in it. The kinds of data and information they collect are not available to anybody else.

Many libraries in the corporate sector are even more heavily into these kinds of programs than we are. So, yes, indeed, there are restrictions—on information, resources, data, and expertise.

Resource sharing. More and more. Do you see that holding down your collection development?

ROSENTHAL: The reality of resource sharing is that a research library may extend its opportunities to tap into more of the world's published and available information in printed or other forms. But it does not allow an institution to curtail its library materials budget.

The pressures from faculty, from library selectors, are such that what you do is to shift from certain areas where you're relying on another institution for comprehensive coverage, and to shift some of the money into areas where your institution is relied upon for comprehensive coverage and where you haven't been achieving that kind of coverage.

The Stanford and Berkeley libraries have allocated certain countries of Latin America to each other for comprehensive coverage. So if we give up Paraguay but take on Peru, we're still going to spend the same amount of money.

GORAL: No. I see it as really positive, mainly because of the lack of materials that we have. We are able to interloan with other agencies throughout the United States for information or materials that they have recorded. It does not inhibit the growth of my own collection. Through the National Library Service we are encouraged to record local materials, so if anyone is interested in Colorado materials, they're available in Colorado. We will gladly send them out to any library for the blind and handicapped.

DUMONT: We're not going to be able to continue to afford the luxury of duplicating knowledge, of duplicating collections everywhere.

What's holding us back from doing more of that are the political struggles between counties and cities and states and universities and community colleges and public libraries and school libraries. There is a lot of parochialism today within each of these institutions.

We have consortia that are working really hard to break down those barriers.

As costs continue to increase, our political entities will be forced to continue to accelerate cooperation if we want to keep up with the knowledge base.

We're really there to serve people. That is what we're supposed to do, and struggles over "turf" between institutions don't help reach that goal.

VASILAKIS: I've seen resource sharing grow and grow and grow and grow. There was a time when it was a lot cheaper to buy a book than it was to try to find it somewhere else. Not so today. OCLC really did a great thing in this area by pioneering that effort.

I see centers of expertise building up in certain subjects. You will always go to the center of expertise for whatever you need. If we get the right copyright clearances, we'll be able to transmit information back and forth easily, quickly, share disks or whatever, telecommunicate and get it to our users a lot faster than we used to be able to.

The objective is not to have the biggest collection; it's to provide the best information. Sometimes you take the money that used to go to buy materials and use it instead to increase your search budget.

ASP: It's awfully hard to think of a library that might be as small as 500 or 600 square feet and maybe have only a couple thousand volumes in it as being capable of producing useful information for a lot of people. I constantly try to remind librarians that they have to emphasize to their users that their building is an access point. Whatever the user's information need is, the library can tap into resources all over the state and all over the country. But if somebody just looks at the quaint little building, it's awfully hard for him or her to realize that it's the front for a structure in a system that's really highly developed for moving information around.

In July 1986, we started total statewide reciprocal borrowing among the public libraries so a person can take his or her public library card and use it in virtually any public library in the state. It's been a tremendous service. It's a wonderful public relations tool because people just love to know that if they're on vacation or traveling around the state they can just run in and check out something from the local library just as if they were at home.

One group that's been very impressed with all this is the state legislature. Our program recognized that they've been investing millions of dollars in library development for the last 30 years or so. Now the structures are strong enough that there can be movement and activity of people around the state using those different kinds of libraries.

There was real reluctance on the part of the large metropolitan libraries to get involved with the statewide reciprocal borrowing program, thinking that folks were going to come in from distant places and check out large numbers of books and maybe not return them. But the total volume is not enough to really be that much of a burden to anybody.

It was taking the plunge, it was being brave enough to make the decision, to try it, to test it; that was the crucial thing. Once we did, it seems to be working out fine.

Chapter 13

Other Changes

This chapter considers: Will your library need structural changes? Why did Dick Dougherty resign? And what are the most important "unfinished business" items in the library field?

———— ◆ ◆ ◆ ————

Do you see structural/architectural changes being necessary in the library?

McDONALD: We are going to have to build with the computer in mind. In a community college, if we designed a library for the year 2000, we would probably have all of our computer labs in one area with a vast media center with learning labs attached. The math department would have its math labs, the English department the English labs, the computer department its labs. This would be a very efficient way to get information to the students, who really just need to be in front of a terminal with someone to help them turn it on and off and give them software.

WHITNEY: As long as you have the capability of reconstructing or reconfiguring electronics in the facility, I don't predict that we're going to be looking at different kinds of structures than we have right now. The basic floor plan in my library is the most usable, flexible facility that I've been in, and this was built in 1968. The architect was wonderful, absolutely wonderful.

We have a lot of open space that we can reconfigure the way we need it. That's the major challenge, to have lots of open space, because visibility is a major problem in a school library, much more so than in any other type of library. We have to maintain visual contact with the kids in the facility. Part of our responsibility is to monitor what goes on.

The architect who designed my facility clearly understood that that was a major factor. We don't have obstructing pillars, and all of the office spaces have windows all the way across so we have visibility wherever we are.

MASON: Until very recently, libraries, because of the expansion of the materials, expected to need new space every 15 years. I don't believe we can keep doing that.

We are planning for a no-growth environment in our physical space. I believe what we will need to do is replace material that is now in print, in book form, with very compact storage capabilities. We'll keep buying in book form for a while, many things. Then we'll go into more compact storage capabilities.

But I don't believe libraries can afford to continue to build buildings every 15 years.

Dick Dougherty, you're leaving your library position. What made you change?

DOUGHERTY: There's no simple answer. And no crisis. I've been doing administration for 16 years—six at Berkeley and 10 at Michigan, and I've just been thinking for some time, what am I going to do for the rest of my lifetime?

The question is, when is a good time? And there never is a good time. This happens to be a year when a number of projects are coming together—it's also the end of my second term as director, my tenth anniversary.

I'm an avid poker player and there are times when you don't throw good money after bad, and then there are times you walk away while you're ahead in the game. It just seemed like a good time. I'm going to leave for seven months and then I'll return to join the faculty of the library school.

I'm interested in what I've come to call library futures. Not just academic libraries, which I hold strong opinions on and where I think I know what's likely to happen, although there will be a whole variety of futures. I'm also interested in the public library. And I'm interested in leadership. I don't know exactly if you can add those all together.

In the last 12 to 18 months, I have listened to a number of people talk about the leadership crisis that exists. There is certainly a lot of attention focused on the topic; the recent LAMA effort in San Antonio and the current ALA effort are two examples. And I think I have something to offer.

I believe the leaders we are seeking are already in the profession. I know an awful lot of people I believe have the potential to become the next generation of leaders. The greatest inhibitors to professional growth are organizational constraints and organizational climate.

My goal is to create a center to address leadership issues. I'm particularly interested in issues such as conflict resolution and risk-taking. I believe it is essential that we create organizational environments in which risk-taking is encouraged and conflict not avoided. It has been my experience that we librarians often seem unwilling to confront problems and often appear to be risk-adverse.

I have also found that we tend to allow disagreements to become personalized. This is not an intended outcome but personalization is often an unwelcome outcome. I have always admired the lawyer's ability to focus disagreements on issues rather than personalities. We too must learn it is not wrong to disagree.

We librarians seem not to be particularly competitive by nature or instinct. However, we are operating in environments and with individuals who are competitive; we must learn to accept competition as a condition of our jobs.

I see many opportunities awaiting the profession in the years ahead, but in order to achieve them the next generation of leaders must be willing to confront conflict and to seize each opportunity as it presents itself.

My dream for the future is to make the school I am associated with undisputedly and undeniably Number One. There isn't any Number One in the country right now. We keep talking about the top five but it's like deciding between Tweedledee and Tweedledum. There is no generally acknowledged leader.

I don't believe there has been a Number One school since the days of the University of Chicago in the late '30s, early '40s, under the leadership of Louis Round Wilson. It was probably the first library school to recruit a number of social scientists to its faculty and they became the authors of the seminal series of studies known as the Public Library Inquiry. It was an extremely influential school and many of the directors who became influential in the post-World War II era you'll find had Ph.D.s from the University of Chicago.

What are the library field's most important "unfinished business" items?

WEDGEWORTH: Do more to encourage research in the field.

There are certain questions that we just don't understand as well as we should. There are certain assumptions that we make without periodically testing them to be sure that we're on sound ground.

So that's one. I think ALA has to recognize that if we're going to push the field to its next height, we've got to have a stronger research base.

For example, we've got to do something about the precise identification of materials that are related to a specific problem. Whether you call it indexing or subject classification, we've got to do more research to develop more precise ways of doing that, and perhaps that are completely different from the key word kind of indexing and subject classification we do now.

This is not something that's going to be solved in general conversation or in the day-to-day operations that we develop to serve users. There's got to be precise and careful study, looking at the various kinds of alternatives that are available to us. We've got to do more research in understanding the impact of technology and understanding the economics of technology.

We've got to make our people very efficient because we'll never have a lot of money, which means we have to use what money we have very well. Our people need to know the tradeoffs in terms of acquiring and using technology, knowing when it's obsolete, when can you write off a particular technology and invest in something else.

There are also going to be managerial questions about personnel. We've developed some completely new organizations in our field where there are very few precedents. And we've broken new ground. For example, universities and school systems are still medieval kingdoms in a twentieth-century world. You can have the world's greatest expert sitting at this university and a host of students at the next university, but there's no natural way to put those two together.

Unfortunately, we don't have the resources to duplicate that kind of competency. And of course talent is not equally distributed across the 50 states of this nation. How long are we going to tolerate that? That doesn't mean that you have uniformly homogeneous institutions, but we need to have ways to create collaborative arrangements.

We have more experience with collaborative arrangements in our field than most of the other areas of education. But that doesn't say that we understand those collaborative organizations as precisely as we should.

We're going to have to do more research to be sure that we understand how to govern effectively and maintain and develop those collaborative organizations in the future. And what kinds of things to avoid.

Another area is that we've got to keep a strong emphasis on documenting what happens currently. It starts fundamentally with statistics. It's shameful that in a country as large and as powerful as ours, we can't say precisely in any given year how many libraries of a given type there are. Or how many people get served by different types of libraries. That kind of information may seem trivial, but it gives you a broad picture of what is going on for which there is very little substitute. The American Library Association has tried to move in that area, but it needs to push harder to get our government to understand that responsibility. It doesn't mean, as they presently interpret it, that the Department of Education has to do the work. The Department of Education has to recognize that the work is important and see to it that the work is distributed in a way that it gets done.

The association has to give real recognition to the contribution and the need for stronger contribution from the professional schools. Professional schools are largely accountable for the quality of people we have out there in the field. If we want people with stronger qualifications, they are more likely to come from those schools than any place else, because while you will get an occasional person from a business school or from a school of public administration, the amount of time and attention that those schools will focus on our field will be minimal.

If we want better people we're going to have to be sure the professional schools understand the need for those people and the obligation and the support that will be necessary to get them. All of those are things that the American Library Association can and should do.

We're also going to have to simplify technologies. We can't afford to have 150 different basic technologies that every single library will have to consider in order to tie into this broad network of services.

We've got to put more emphasis on kinds of omnibus front ends where each library would acquire the same front end, but will give them access to any and all the basic kinds of technologically based services that are available there to assist our users.

Why should you have a front end A in New York and front end B in Los Angeles and front end C in Toronto and front end D in Dallas, and we're all scrambling to get enough people to join our system so that we can be sure that we can get access to them. It doesn't make sense.

That's where the Association can come in. To set standards. To be sure that these systems are compatible and that we don't drive up the cost for our constituents simply because we don't have compatible systems of technology for serving the users.

All of those things are important for the American Library Association and the other major associations to be involved in.

WHITNEY: Many times librarians are so overwhelmed with the day-to-day operation of the facility, we get so involved in cataloging the collection and dealing with students on an individual basis that we don't see the big picture. And I think it's really incumbent upon the national association to try to provide that perspective, to try to encourage people to step back and look at the overall picture and determine what's their primary priority, and go after that and let some of the details slide for a while for the greater good.

EASTMAN: Although we have extraordinary technology and extraordinary access to information, we also have 23 million adults in this country—most of whom have graduated from the public school system—who cannot read.

That's a tragedy. It's also a great danger to all the rest of us. And if we can't solve the literacy problem pretty quickly, and keep it from compounding exponentially as more and more high school graduates can't read, there isn't much point in talking about how they're going to access information because they aren't going to be able to use it at all.

That's frightening because their only source of information will be radio, television, and oral communication. They can't broaden their horizons by pursuing in more depth the topics that books, magazines, newspapers, and media of all kinds present.

It's also frightening because these people vote. One reason I've always been such a strong library supporter is that I believe that people who vote on issues should seek pertinent information. They also borrow and use books and other materials for other reasons but find there information that influences the way they vote, the way they think about the quality of life.

And the whole field needs to improve public relations. It becomes more and more clear to me, after a lifetime of working in the public relations and fundraising areas for libraries, that we have not been very successful. PR isn't just what you see—the tea parties, the posters, National Library Week. PR is a state of mind, a reaching out to the uninformed. Done successfully, it permeates every aspect of library service. Each library worker can test his or her effect on public relations by asking such simple questions as, "How, ultimately, does what I'm doing affect users, and how can I get that message across?"

We need to get much better at telling people who pay the bills, whoever they are (vice-presidents for information or provosts, college presidents, public library boards, school boards) why it is that library service is essential to the quality of life in this country, and why it has to be paid for. We need to explain better that professional human beings provide services, that those services are not clerical work, and that libraries are not storehouses.

A library is a very special kind of institution that has its own synergy and in some cases also its own entropy. What is done in one department vastly impacts what's done in another department to provide an overall service package to every user who walks through that door.

We are not explaining to people who need to know—political figures and others who control budgets—why library service is so essential in our society, and why a library is a unique place. One can't possibly have at home access to all the information one may need.

There is also a proliferation of organizations in the library community, so now you can't go, say, to ALA and SLA and assume you have pretty fully checked out whatever question you have about the state of librarianship in this country today. Today you must talk to all these people who run networks around the country—to the Association of Research Libraries, to the OCLC users group, to many others.

Librarians are constantly meeting in different, smaller, and more specialized groups. Much of this change is brought about by the advent of technology. But they aren't, therefore, communicating about the larger issues of what really is happening in this country to the philosophy of library service and to librarianship.

If librarians lose—or don't develop—the ability to articulate these and other larger concerns among themselves, how can they expect to be effective in doing so with nonlibrarians, especially those who control budgets at all administrative levels?

And a last plea:

One of the real sources of ineffective leadership in the library field is poor communication. We have fallen into reliance on dead nouns, the passive voice, and boiler plate language.

One reason people pay so little attention to what is written in library literature is that it is often poorly written. If the author isn't sufficiently interested in what he or she is doing to make it interesting to the reader, what is going to motivate the reader to pay attention? If more librarians thought what they had done was important and interesting, they couldn't help but communicate that fact when they speak and write. Some of our communications lack class and style—and a little style never hurt anyone.

I would like to see ALA make a concerted effort to improve its administrative communications (I exempt from this statement the promotional materials produced by the Public Information Office, which are uniformly excellent). Think of the hours and dollars we could save in Council meetings if we didn't have to argue about what a resolution means. Ambiguities should be resolved before more than 100 people try to deal with the language.

Chapter 14

Congressman Major R. Owens

The only librarian in the U.S. Congress sees more massive funding for libraries, including financing of a bold new concept he calls the Family Learning Center. At the right time he plans to introduce legislation to support a half billion to a billion dollar five-year demonstration project to wipe out illiteracy. In this endeavor he considers public libraries more important than public schools. He also has some suggestions for the Library and the Librarian of Congress.

———— ♦ ♦ ♦ ————

What are the prospects for the library community in 1998, 10 years from now, from the standpoint of the federal relationship?

OWENS: I think that any institution that is connected with education has a great future. That may be hard to believe because the present is so difficult, and the past has not demonstrated that the power structure and the people who make decisions about how to allocate the money have any great faith in the contribution libraries make and can make.

But I think we're in the situation where the rhetoric about education being important is slowly being overtaken by the reality that education really is very important and it has been neglected. We are in the position of becoming a second-class power or a crippled first-class power, the leader of the free world but definitely crippled by the fact that we have neglected and grossly mutilated our education system.

Every institution which has some relationship with education will have a place of priority in the coming future. We will discover as we try to work our way out of a national anti-intellectual milieu—our frame of reference in this country is anti-intellectual—we're going to discover that we have to saturate the environment with educational activities, and we have to boost everything that promotes education.

Reading certainly promotes it. Starting from illiteracy, at every level you need help with basic literacy. You also need to greatly increase the amount of information available to people who know how to use information, greatly increase the stimulation in our intellectual atmosphere. All along the way in every one of those particular kinds of activities, you're going to find libraries will prove very useful. How soon they become involved and how deeply they become involved will depend on leadership within the library profession.

That leadership is certainly burned-out and disillusioned. It's going to take some fresh leadership, I think, to seize the initiative when the opportunity presents itself. I'm not talking about five years from now, I'm talking about something happening in the next two or three years.

Even the present Administration recognizes that it has been long on rhetoric with respect to education and short on substance and will have to begin to make some effort to compensate for that. You're going to first find more media posturing about education and gimmickry, people appearing to solve the problem by latching on to some highly visible, sexy gimmicks and special projects. That's going to be the beginning of a whole explosion of support. It's going to move from that gimmickry to some real support for activities like libraries.

You've got to have literacy; you've got to have the attitude that reading is the key. The age of electronics has not negated the necessity of developing competency in reading, of understanding the printed word. Everybody who's a leader anywhere is a reader. The people who produce the electronic magic are readers. The habits of our population, the habits of our young people are all formed through the kinds of activities you can produce related to education as they are growing up and within that community.

We need what I call Family Learning Centers. Public libraries—I would like to see some converted into Family Learning Centers where everybody in the family can come.

You have computers in the library so that people who can never afford to have a computer in their home can come and practice and deal with that, but they also bring the whole family so that the little kids are reading in the children's room, and the mother is dealing with whatever, probably her job, since most mothers are working nowadays.

All of that is taking place under one roof, and they see the library as being the place they can go to and get the kind of help they could never afford on their own.

If you're talking about massive upgrading of massive amounts of people, how do you make the right kind of help available to them? The library becomes the place where you can reach all segments of the population and on a regular basis.

And if you create a different atmosphere and you put some video machines in the library to do some how-to stuff on the videos in the how-to section for books, overnight you'll see there will be an increase in the number of persons using the library.

For example, how to take a civil service test—you run, every other hour, a video on it. People can come, look at the book, and you've sold the book. Yes, let's go in to selling books. We've got a big financial operation in libraries anyhow; just collecting the fines has created a financial system. Every branch has a money-collecting system, so let's sell books. Bookstores are closing rapidly, especially in the big cities.

A person can go to the library and get a generalized explanation on a video, look at some books there, look at the one that best suits him or her and then buy one to take home. That's a critical point in their lives when they're trying to pass the civil service test. I know from my work in branches how it happens, how they come in, all at once.

Do you see ever again the big money for libraries from the U.S. Congress?

OWENS: Yes I do. Yes I do. The library is in a position to get it from several points. We talk a lot about illiteracy, but we never put enough money behind it to mean anything. It's about time we put money behind it.

The one institution that is likely to get the bulk of any money that's put into a real drive to try to wipe out illiteracy will be the public libraries.

You're going to need a crusade. We're at the point now where it's going to break. The Congress will also recognize the role of libraries in elementary and secondary education. And the role of libraries in college education.

Your vision is that there will be great Congressional support, great federal support, for libraries before the year 2000?

OWENS: Definitely.

What should go into that program—support for literacy training and what other specifics?

OWENS: The concept that is most needed and would also get the best response is the library as a Family Learning Center. That's where we start by financing some demonstration projects to convert—it's not really converting libraries, it's really supplementing what they do now—by putting in more educational hardware, computers, video machines, and deal with what are the needs of a particular kind of community at every age group level.

No matter how poor a community is in New York City, for example, there are a large number of college students in that community because education can be obtained at a relatively low cost—not low enough, but there are some college students there.

There also are always large numbers of civil servants in our communities—large numbers of people who are either trying to get employment in the state government or the federal government or the city government. Adults who need help with civil service tests are always there.

There are a large number of people who need retraining because of the rapid changes in our economy and industries. There are always children who are in high school, and elementary and secondary school, and preschool. And there are always parents. Every library should better serve all of those, not with just the traditional formats, the printed words, but let's get a more practical program because the printed word is not always the best way to teach people who are just learning. It's the way that they expand on their education after they're taught.

To lead people into a literacy program you need more audiovisual materials. You also need the format people are the most comfortable with. Everybody watches television; there's a magic to that. We should put more money into television.

For how long should this be financed?

OWENS: The political realities are that you could probably get five-year financing of demonstration projects and not much more than that. And I think in five years we would know enough to be able to go forward or to call for funding from other sources.

What kind of funding will be appropriate at the beginning?

OWENS: A concept like the Family Learning Center I'd want to have heavily duplicated. I'd want some in urban areas, but not one urban area, 20 urban areas. I'd want some in rural areas, and some with high concentrations of senior citizens. I'd want to see it in every state, every major city. My concept would not be 10 or 15 projects, but between 50 to 75.

We need to learn a lot and we need to learn it fast and we should move on that scale.

Moneywise, here's where the leadership in Congress, my education and labor committee, here's where we have to make some breakthroughs and provide the leadership to make our colleagues understand the twentieth-century financing for education and libraries.

They were forced to understand it in the area of the military. If 50 years ago you'd have talked about representatives in Congress ever voting 3.5 billion dollars to produce an aircraft carrier, they would have told you you were crazy. Weapons systems have taught us what modern expenditures are all about.

Fortunately, when you start talking about education, you're not talking about anything in that league. You give me what an aircraft carrier costs and I'll fund education for the next 10 years. I'll fund the libraries for the next 10 years. In the entire existence of the Library Services Construction Act, they haven't spent enough to cover one aircraft carrier.

We have to make a breakthrough and say, look, we need real money to put in every library an adequate set of computers for people to train on, video machines, movies, something that they can really work with. Plus the funding for a technician full-time so when that stuff starts breaking down somebody's there to fix it. We need money to put in there what you really need, and personnel to back up the librarians.

You don't send a nuclear submarine out with the kind of staffing that submarines had 20 years ago. You send it out with what it costs nowadays. So let's talk about the funding that's needed.

The problem so far is that we refuse to propose what's really needed and we move at incremental steps and we undercut our own activities. For instance, computers in the school. Everybody recognizes you've got to have computer education, but throughout most of this country computers in the schools are a farce. Except for a few situations, you have the hardware there and nobody knows how to use it properly and they don't have the backup to fix them, to repair them. The minute they break down they're down for weeks and months at a time.

A young intern on my staff did a survey and he found that a year after computer components had been purchased, most of them were locked up somewhere in a closet, or in safekeeping, because the teachers and principals are worried so much more about security than anything else. They'd given up trying to use them. You can't field this new technology, which is in many ways necessary, and can get the job done, without proper support staff, without paying the price.

Now, to launch demonstration projects in the next two or three years, you're talking about doing it right, you need between half a billion or a billion dollars, to really do it right.

What do library leaders need to do to get ready to help with that kind of a program?

OWENS: The first thing that library leaders need to do is to correct the present mind set. The present mind set of librarians and library leaders has been shaped by the very bad eight years of Ronald Reagan.

The economy is scarcity, the atmosphere is scarcity, and it has created a situation where we glorify the virtues of being able to do more with less, to hold on. We really don't want to hear a lot of talk about innovations and expansions, we don't want to hear any dreams.

We have to recognize that we are going forward into a situation where there's going to be recognition of the need for education at every level and that there's no way to meet the demands that are going to be placed on the library when that recognition hits through the traditional methods of providing library service.

There's nothing wrong with our basic approaches, we are just going to have to be able, willing to expand and supplement the kinds of activities we do and understand that we're in the age of technology and make maximum use of the technology that is available.

The public's imagination has to be captured. People who are illiterate still are not going to stay in a course unless there's some kind of excitement there. Just the recognition that they need to learn to read is not enough; you've got to use the best techniques available to capture their attention, their motivation.

And all of that means that we're going to have to have leaders who have a broad perception of what it's all about. The interdisciplinary orientation of libraries and public library systems and branch libraries and so forth; it's going to have to be there.

They have to understand what educators are doing, what the larger world of education is all about. Understand what's going on with job training. Understand what welfare reform means, when welfare reform says we're going to force all women who have kids who are two or three years old or older to go to work if they want to stay on welfare.

And go to work means that first they are required by the legislation that passed the Congress recently to report to a counselor and get into an educational program. Well, that person may be at an eighth-grade reading level. Who's going to provide the education that's going to bring them up to a level where they can take the next step and go into a job training program? Is there a role for libraries there?

Librarians and library leaders have to know about what that's all about and how to offer themselves in that process. In large cities, library buildings are located within walking distance of a lot of these people. There's no other institution that's free to do that kind of job or located so well.

Library buildings in large cities often have space that's not being fully utilized. There are a number of ways that they can begin immediately to meet some of these needs for adult education and literacy education and pretraining for jobs. And they have to be available. The mentality has to be that this is part of what we should be doing.

The library will be more important than the schools because public schools have a job to do that they have not done. The great failure has been that they haven't done the job they were set up to do, so they really shouldn't be taking on any extra activities.

Public schools have got to find out how to educate kids. Too many illiterate people today have gone to school. We don't want them to keep turning out people who really haven't been educated up to the level where schools are supposed to bring them. We don't want them to keep allowing so many youngsters to escape out of the system because of the school's inability to cope with certain kinds of backgrounds, with certain kinds of problems.

Libraries running literacy programs may run out of space and they may have to contract with schools for after-school space. School space is the primary thing that public schools could offer to any program, because they are underutilized. The plants and facilities are only utilized for a small period of the day, so that's always a possibility.

But in the running of these programs, libraries can do certain parts far better than public schools and should step forward and lay aside the fear of getting burned, as they have been in the past, where you start programs and get involved in them, and then they cut off the funding. Or you run into problems that libraries are not used to having with the community participation. The faint-hearted should step aside and let people who are a little more willing risk problems and provide leadership.

You have introduced into Congress a bill about the Librarian of Congress position, right?

OWENS: Yes. You need high visibility in this society in order to be recognized and accorded the role that is your due. And if you have the Librarian of Congress being chosen from people other than librarians for that pinnacle position of the library profession, something is very wrong.

The Solicitor General must be a person learned in the law, Congressional legislation says. They don't say they'll take lawyers only, but you let somebody who's learned in law who's not a lawyer try to become Solicitor General. Or go to the Supreme Court. There's no requirement that a Supreme Court judge must be a lawyer, but they always go to the Bar Association and if you can't get a rating by the bar, then you can forget it.

So, it's important to take over that highly visible pinnacle in Washington and let it be known that here is the library profession, and the Librarian of Congress really ought to know librarianship. The man who's there now, I have no complaints, he's an intellectual, he's a scholar, but he's not a librarian and there are a thousand things that he needs to know about and should make priorities that he won't ever make a priority because he just doesn't understand.

The Library of Congress is obsolete as it functions now. It should be not viewed any more as a building or a set of buildings, it ought to be viewed as a system and you should have collections of the Library of Congress spread throughout the country, with collections that already exist.

Vanderbilt University has an excellent Civil War collection from the point of view of the Confederacy. Brooklyn Public Library has an excellent Civil War collection from the point of view of the Union. Three or four collections like that about the Civil War should be certified as Library of Congress collections and the Library of Congress should stop trying to be the only authority on the Civil War.

The authority on Hawaii should be the Hawaii State Library. Let's stop collecting material in Washington, the rare books about old Hawaii and all that stuff; let it stay at home. But let it be certified as a Library of Congress collection and if they need federal funds to keep the books in certain condition, to recatalog them in a certain way so that scholars can easily have access to them, let's give it to them.

You know, let us do those things in terms of systems. It is far more efficient economically, and effective in terms of use, than the present system where we have a warehousing mentality. We're looking for more and more space in Washington to put more and more books that are harder to get.

The new Librarian of Congress, he doesn't know what I was talking about when I was talking about systems. So the profession has made a major mistake in not seizing the initiative behind me on this one.

Chapter 15

Deputy Librarian of Congress William Welsh

Here the man who knows more than anyone else about this greatest institution of its kind reports how far the LC has come on its multitiered preservation program and predicts that, for the year 2000, "we'll have the solution organized." He also details just how wrenching the process of determining who will decide book by book what to save and what to throw away can be. Another topic: What the LC will be doing for the nation's libraries by the end of the next decade and—since this is a two-way street—what the nation's libraries can be doing for the LC.

———— ♦ ♦ ♦ ————

What's going to be happening at the LC between now and 2000?

WELSH: The year 2000 will be the 200th anniversary of the Library of Congress. We have been giving much thought to that in a number of areas, particularly in space, which for us is a very critical problem.

That fine Jefferson building was opened in 1897, the Adams building was opened in 1938, and we began to occupy this large Madison building in 1980. But we discovered in 1986 that by the year 1992, we will need more space for at least our book collections.

A library, in a way unlike any other institution in the world, needs to grow, to add more space. The rate of growth is the only factor that's in question. Right now, we see a need for additional linear feet of shelving to accommodate about 3 million volumes.

Those 3 million volumes represent 10 years of growth in our book collections.

We are, as you know, working diligently in the field of optical disk technology. We know there's enormous compaction in that technology, but we're not sure how we should apply it because preservation is the more immediate problem we have to face.

Of the 84 million items in our collections, there are 13 million books, over 25% of which are embrittled. We've got to microfilm those books, since there's no other technology that's available to satisfy that need. The deacidification technology will solve the problem of extending the life of books.

Ninety-seven percent of all the printed materials in the Library contain acid. Almost all the material coming into the Library from every place in the world contains acid.

Our plan is to deacidify on a mass scale all incoming materials and then eventually, over a 20-year period, deacidify all the nonbrittle books in our collections. We also know that in the process we are going to keep millions of books in their original format, so we've got to provide for them. We know we're going to microfilm 3 million books and that will save a lot of space.

We are working with others to try to get publishers to produce their library materials on acid-free paper. The number of plants that produce acid-free paper has increased dramatically; there are 13 or 14 now. Still acid-free paper is not widely used. But less than 2% of the paper produced in this country ends up in libraries, so we're not a great market for acid-free paper, but we're still working on it. More than half of the materials we acquire are produced in foreign lands where wood pulp paper, which causes the problem, is used almost without exception.

We have a number of approaches to satisfy the preservation problem: microfilming for the embrittled books, diethyl zinc treatment for those materials that can be treated by that process, and optical disk for current serials. Those approaches give us some clues about where we're going to be in the year 2000.

A number of people believe that we can be a paperless society. I'm not one who shares that view. There are a lot of good, old-fashioned reasons that we ought to continue to have the book.

Some changes are taking place. Every day we see more evidence of machine-readable copy. Many of the reference books that have been hardbound copy in the past are now in machine-readable form. Audio-visual materials are increasing very, very rapidly.

The role of the library will essentially remain the same in the year 2000; that is, we will have to be the custodian of the machine-readable records as well as other formats. I don't believe the private sector is going to have any interest in maintaining unprofitable back files.

There is a new problem that relates to machine-readable material. With many of the reference tools coming in now in that format, you're asked when you subscribe to a new edition or update to send the former edition back to the publisher, which means the record of the past is no longer readily available to us as it is now. We will have to play a role in that to decide what out-of-date reference tools ought to be kept.

The bigger problem that I see in preservation is what to save. There are a lot of anecdotes about that, but I recall one time several years ago when Mortimer Adler was here having lunch.

I posed the question to him, "What should we save?"

And he said, "Well, that's too difficult a question. Why don't we address what we should throw away?"

I said, "Fine."

He said, "How about the Zane Grey novels?"

I wasn't sure that he was serious and I said, "Well, how do you feel about *The Bobbsey Twins on a Houseboat?*"

He didn't respond.

I said, "How about the Sears and Roebuck catalog?"

He said, "Why would anyone want to keep the Sears and Roebuck catalog?"

I said, "Well, for our purposes it's a great record of our culture, so there's a good and sufficient reason to keep it."

We talked to a number of distinguished scholars on the subject of what to save and it seems that it's almost an impossible question to answer.

I asked the Catholic archbishop here in Washington, "What in the field of religious publications would you save?"

That's a complicated question because there are some organizations that keep certain types of their own publications, but we don't even know for certain how many religions there are in the whole world, nor for that matter how many languages there are in the whole world. So the challenge for us in the library world generally is to decide collectively what we ought to save and keep forevermore.

If, for example, there were a holocaust, what would we wish to preserve? I've wondered, what is the role of the Smithsonian in keeping a record of our past? In the printed area, should there be a complementary role for the Library of Congress? We're the generation that is going to play a major role in preservation because we're going to have to say, item by item, what we're going to save.

By the year 2000, you can expect some changes but we're still going to be working with library-like materials and performing library-like functions. As far as I can see, we'll be doing just that forevermore.

What will be the role of the library in society in the year 2000?

WELSH: The role won't have changed. We should become much more active, much more aggressive in providing service and information to all users, whether it be to the commercial sector, the government, or the private citizen.

We've got to do more than just supply the race track enthusiasts with their records; we've got to be able to provide records to people who are interested in tracing their genealogy, to people who want to know about the stock market, information to answer all sorts of questions.

We ought to be the central information source. The small public library becomes as important as the major research library. The poor need to be served. Maybe we ought to have a program of literacy stamps, like food stamps, to make sure that the poor or less fortunate are served. We need to serve the rural populations more effectively than we have. Our role is essentially that of the guardian of the past and provider of information wherever it's needed.

Are there books in the Library of Congress that cannot be microfilmed, that cannot be deacidified?

WELSH: All books can be microfilmed; the problem is that it's so costly. It costs on the average about $60 to microfilm a single volume.

As far as I know, we haven't really lost a single volume. Most of our material that is in bad shape will stand one more use. And the one more use is for microfilming, so I think that you can microfilm up to a certain level and then beyond that you deacidify and you use other formats as well.

Of course, those are just stop-gap measures. We don't know what the configuration of a fourth or fifth or sixth building for the Library of Congress ought to be. I'm convinced that such a building will not be built here on Capitol Hill. The space here on Capitol Hill is at a premium, so I think we're looking at remote storage to address our space problems, although maybe not to solve them.

What will the Library of Congress be doing for the nation's libraries in the year 2000?

WELSH: Essentially what we're doing now:

One, providing cataloging information. Our principal function is providing the standards by which cataloging information is transmitted. We have the largest staff of experts in subjects and language or symbol in the world working to provide cataloging information. So we ought to be communicating with the utilities—OCLC and RLG—providing them copy, doing it more rapidly than we're now able to do it.

Two, there are 57 million items in our collection that are nonprint. Much of the material is unique. We have a responsibility to transmit to libraries everywhere the knowledge contained in those collections.

Three, we have to share our resources and that's really the bottom line—the sharing of resources. We have to play a central role in sharing of resources. There's no point in collecting materials that are not going to be used.

You said, do it more rapidly. How rapidly?

WELSH: Immediately for some things. With online communication we can do that now.

On optical disk, you can just sit down before a terminal, use the bibliographic tools to locate the item, whether it's in *The New York Times* or *Congressional Record*, and immediately call on a screen the very document you're looking for. If you want a print-out, then you can print it out on a convenience printer.

We ought to be able to do that across-the-board. In one sense, in a program called "Cataloging in Publication" we are doing that.

We get from publishers of U.S. trade materials the bibliographic data before the publication is actually printed. We do the cataloging immediately, so when that book is printed the cataloging information is in the book.

But we ought to be better. For example, we're getting in today 6,000 pieces. We ought to be able to catalog those pieces much more rapidly. Turnaround time ought to be three to four days. Perhaps it's an impossible dream, but it ought to be done more promptly.

How long is the time today?

WELSH: We have a system of priorities so the English-language material gets first priority in cataloging and then down the line, which means that some of the materials never get out of the shop. The system was designed that way. If the need for certain material is identified, you can retrieve it and change the priorities, but the average time for processing can be months.

What could the libraries of the country do for the Library of Congress? Is it a two-way street?

WELSH: Oh yes, absolutely.

They can work with us to produce cataloging data according to a national standard and so take the burden off of us of doing more of the original cataloging. There is movement in this direction now and that seems to be very, very reassuring.

In the field of preservation we need to develop a national plan, and there's a Commission on Preservation and Access that's working toward that in the embrittled book program so that if one university is preserving something, the Library of Congress does not need to do it. Nobody else does, either.

By the year 2000, will preservation still be a problem?

WELSH: I think it will be a problem, but we'll have the solution organized. We won't be able to do it all. For example, as I said, our diethyl zinc deacidification program is a 20-year program, but the technology works and we know the system that we set up works. We won't have done it all, but we'll have it organized and we can go on to something else.

Was the technology revolution oversold in libraries?

WELSH: I don't think it's been oversold. I think the problem is that there's more technology out there than we know how to deal with at this time. In the field of optical disk, we were the first to apply this technology to a library situation, so private industry had to try to keep up with us, with what our needs are. The CD-ROM technology, for example, has far outreached our ability to apply it.

The proportion of books that you keep—was it at one time really 100%?

WELSH: It never was 100%. We have always been highly selective. There's an enormous amount of material that comes in through copyright deposit, and even though we have 84 million items, that represents literally the cream of the crop of materials that are available.

We're more selective in some areas than others. For example, we were much more comprehensive in our selection of phonograph records until recently; now, we have tightened our selection policy. Some criteria are dictated by the budget crunch, others by just an opportunity to evaluate what we're selecting.

What are the criteria for evaluation?

WELSH: Generally, scholarly use is our first criterion, but there's no simple answer to that question. We have an acquisition policy statement which amounts to about a foot high of materials. It varies considerably. For example, it's highly specific in some areas. In newspapers, I can tell you exactly what newspapers we collect from every city in the world.

In the case of Bulgarian poetry, it's much more a matter of judgment. You can argue late into the night about how many copies you need of Bulgarian poetry published in 1879, versus Estonian fiction in some other year.

Fiction is another area for such judgment. We do acquire a considerable amount of fictional works. We have certain authors that we collect comprehensively. But you can also raise questions: How many copies of every one of Louis L'Amour's books should be kept? Should we keep each one of his titles? He's a favorite author of mine, but he's what some people describe as a formula writer.

He has three favorite topics he writes about, but do you need everything he's written about the West? Now some people will argue, yes, you do, because if you want to do a study of the West you could not do it without Louis L'Amour. Louis L'Amour has a collection of 8,000 books in his own home in his own library, so he's done an awful lot of basic research.

It's been argued recently with me that we should not keep teen pornography. This is from a moral, religious point of view. My response is that that might be true from a religious, moral point of view, but if someone wants to study this strange phenomenon, the only way you can do that is by looking at the collections of the library.

Some people might argue that we shouldn't be keeping statistics. In the local situation here we have something like 44 murders in just five weeks so far this year. This is the highest by far, ever. Somebody's got to use those figures to decide what's happened here.

So it's pretty hard to judge today what will be useful tomorrow. You've got to use your judgment the best you can.

When you decide what to throw away, are you then second-guessing the judgment that was made initially?

WELSH: As a matter of fact, our premise is that our first judgment was pretty good.

We have a staff of recommending officers, over 100, who look at the current materials, and we periodically review our collection. But, primarily, what we're throwing away are multiple copies of works that we have collected.

Even something as prestigious as the *Library Journal*—we get 35 copies and you obviously don't need to save all of them. One copy will be enough.

You do go back not to rethink it but more likely to fill in gaps. You say, well here's an area where we didn't collect as comprehensively as we should, so then we seek to get materials.

We established, I think it was about 1948, a policy of acquiring materials comprehensively in all subjects in all areas of the world in all languages. And there's an anecdote that relates to that.

I was summoned over to the Librarian's office, along with my boss, to account for why we were collecting Burmese materials when the Librarian said we don't have anybody on the staff who knows Burmese.

My boss answered, "When you have somebody who needs it, we'll have the material."

That policy was then confirmed; we now collect materials comprehensively with the expectation that the retrospective problem will not be so serious as it has been in the past.

Generally, except for the country of Albania, we've been very successful. We've acquired materials from Cuba and from Iran even at a time when negotiations were very, very limited. We have a good reputation around the world of acquiring materials for scholars.

What's the problem with Albania?

WELSH: Pretty much a closed society. They simply don't allow much communication with the other world.

Do they do much publishing?

WELSH: We're not sure about that. We don't really know a lot about it. Obviously there's some.

Censorship. Is there going to be more of it?

WELSH: I don't think so. I think there's an awareness. There will be problems in the courts, the local school boards will decide a policy, and I suppose on a personal level I would like to see a lot more things be decided on a local level. Maybe that sort of thing should be decided on a local level rather than on a national level.

We've always had this sort of discussion. I don't see any evidence of it increasing.

You're the most knowledgeable person about the greatest institution of its kind. What part of your dream for this marvelous place will NOT be accomplished by the year 2000?

WELSH: I suppose maybe the whole realization about what the Library of Congress ought to be. If I have a concern, it's that we are so busy in running this place and running our lives that there's not enough time to think. There are all these administrative problems in running a shop of 5,000 employees and a budget of a quarter of a billion dollars. We don't have the time to do creative thinking, to think sufficiently about the future.

What is the report of the Library of Congress going to say of the year 2000?

WELSH: It will show that we've reexamined our missions again, confirmed that our first responsibility is to Congress; second, to the nation's libraries; third, to the scholarly public; and fourth, to the protection of the creative rights of this nation. It's difficult to view those missions changing in any dramatic way.

Our biggest department still is the processing department. That's the department that supplies the cataloging data. Even with all the advantages of technology it's important to remember that without our staff of experts in subjects and languages, the country couldn't operate as efficiently.

We have the greatest pool of linguistic expertise here we can track or train. We'll have finished the renovation of the Jefferson building and that's going to be a monument to some of us who had the courage to believe that that building must live on. I think it's the finest building, certainly one of the most beautiful buildings in the whole world. The other, newer buildings of the Library are simply more functional, but that one is a monument.

Another item the report will include is that we, fortunately, had 3 million visitors in the year 2000—people who were brought in to show them something about the library. We'll have better exhibits. A visit to the Library of Congress will give them a better understanding of their culture and their background. It will also show them new technology at work. What that technology will be remains to be seen.

It's also going to report that we continue to serve the Congress. Maybe we will have helped to solve the budget process for the Congress, because that's one of the problems that plagues us as users of appropriations. Maybe we'll have found a way to provide information to all the members of Congress, to satisfy all of their needs.

What we do in the Congressional Research Service now is anticipate the new issues. We've got documents that show what are the pros and cons of the major issues confronting us. Maybe we won't have settled the problem of aid to Nicaragua or solved the Contra problems. Maybe those things will continue.

I said in my first trip to China in 1979, that if the Chinese and the Americans used libraries and learned about each other's culture through the libraries, the barriers that separate us would be knocked down. I believe that now.

Chapter 16

Frederick Kilgour

This library giant, whose ingenuity and inventiveness drastically re-made the library world, came into prominence almost exactly a century after Melvil Dewey—and had at least
as much impact. In this wide-ranging interview, he reveals
intimate details of how he started with the original OCLC,
why his new EIDOS will "wreck" the present OCLC, what
libraries must do for users in order to survive to the year
2000, and some of his personal plans for the future.

———— ♦ ♦ ♦ ————

First it was the Ohio College Library Center, right?

KILGOUR: It really all started back in July of 1876, when
Professor Otis H. Robinson, librarian at the University of Roches-
ter, gave a paper at a meeting in Albany in which he reported that
he visited several large libraries in New England and found that
catalogers everywhere were cataloging the same books that were
being cataloged in his place, and he wanted to see some way to cut
out the duplication of effort.

Well, for 90 years after that, librarians kept talking about how
to cut down on the duplication. Back in 1877, librarians got the
idea that the publishers ought to do the cataloging and have it in
the book and then they could just take it out of the book. R.R.
Bowker, a publisher who certainly was a great friend to the
librarians, told them that they had to understand that publishing
was a business, not a philanthropy.

But this is typical of what librarians do. Their view of
cooperation is that you and I do something together and it costs
you money but it doesn't cost me any money, you see.

In 1901, the Library of Congress began to make its own
catalog cards available for a small fee. Essentially it was selling its
cataloging and so to a considerable extent, cut down this duplication of work.

It was just 70 years later that OCLC began to operate, in 1971. There had been this long history of librarians wanting to do some kind of a cooperative business to cut down duplication of cataloging work, so I didn't have to do any market analysis. It was there in the literature and I had been aware of it for a long time.

What was the kernel of the original OCLC idea?

KILGOUR: The campus presidents in Ohio had had a recommendation from a consultant for a traditional, classical bibliographic center, but Ralph Parker and I, as later consultants, told them that that was no time to be traditional.

We suggested that they use a centralized computerization of libraries that would both cut down on the cost and would automatically build a union catalog, which was the major thing they were interested in. They wanted to make the materials in Ohio college and university libraries available to individuals, particularly students, at individual institutions, because they were introducing into undergraduate education programs of independent study, and they knew that they could never have independent college libraries that could support such programs.

It was really the presidents that brought the original OCLC into being. Librarians never would have done it. And looking to the future, what's going to bring EIDOS into being is the users of information, not librarians.

What was there about the original OCLC that attracted you?

KILGOUR: Well, I will wager you that at least 100 people said to me after I came to Columbus, why did you ever leave Yale? You're not supposed to leave a place like that. I told them that I didn't leave Yale, that I went to Columbus. Furthermore, I got computer terminals into the Yale University library a sight faster by going to Columbus than I would have by staying in New Haven.

I grew up in New England and I was familiar with New England, but New England at that time was a very conservative place. I always give an example to illustrate this. The first loan that I negotiated with a bank here in Columbus was for some random access memory equipment. After the vice-president and I had signed for the loan, the vice-president asked me, if we had to foreclose on this equipment, what could we use it for?

I said, sorry, but you couldn't use it for anything.

However, in New England, that question would have been asked before signing and I never would have gotten the loan. That's the difference; the Midwest is more innovative minded.

Columbus, for it must be 15 years now, has been the world center of online, interactive computation with CompuServe here, OCLC, *Chemical Abstracts*, Battelle, and the Ohio State University Libraries. There are also large firms in Columbus, like American Electric Power and Bordens, that have big internal online systems.

But the main thing in the case here is people. Bankers and just plain people are more interested in innovation here than in any other part of the country, or they certainly were at that time, and they were prepared to support calculated risks. That's why OCLC happened here.

I came out here for an interview at a time when I was being considered for the directorship of libraries at another Ivy League university, and the main reason I came out here was that the fellow who asked me was such a nice guy I felt I'd be rude if I didn't come. So I came and I came to play for real. I had my speech all prepared. I asked for a salary that I knew had to be higher than some of the college presidents; it wasn't all that high, it was $27,000.

I met with the committee in the morning, and after we had lunch I went to the OSU computer center to see if I could work with them and if they were interested in working with me. It turned out that they were.

When I came back to the main campus to see the committee, they offered me the job. They had called the absent members and they'd approved, so I decided that if these guys can move that fast, this is probably the place for me. So that was how that came about.

What have you not done through OCLC that you hoped you could have?

KILGOUR: There were two things. You know when you get on in your own professional career, the time comes when you set a target or two to achieve before you really quit. I set two targets:

One was to participate in bringing about a national network, an online network for libraries. Well, I did more than participate, I actually brought it about.

The other was to develop a system for the computerization of cataloging that wouldn't involve people at all. I haven't done that yet, but I could do it in six months right now with the development of books in electronic form. It would be easy.

So I intend to get that second thing done. But it's going to wreck the present OCLC. OCLC has gotten up onto a plateau, and it has begun to tip down a little bit because of a lot of competition. OCLC's got to find a new way to earn its way in the world.

Now let me tell you another thing before we go further. I started to do a paper about the evolution of the book. The book came into being about 2500 B.C. in both Sumer and Egypt. The Egyptian development was on paper rolls, papyrus rolls. The next development was in the second century A.D., when Christians invented the Codex book.

About 1,200 years later in 1450, printing was developed and went like wildfire, and I know why. It was just the same as OCLC. People really wanted a lot more stuff to read and use than they had and printing just exploded. It was like tossing a match into some spilled gasoline.

Then 500 years later, the electronic book comes along and we're right in the early stage of that one. The electronic book is surely going to have the same experience as the printed book.

Are you familiar with the fairly recently developed concept of punctuated equilibria in evolutionary thinking? Well, the idea here is that you have periods in paleontological time, during which a lot of species become extinct and a lot of others come into being. Then you have relative stability for quite a while and then another period of change.

This same thing went on with the book. For 500 years, the book really hasn't changed. As I see it, we're really right in the beginning of a revolution that isn't just a library revolution; it's a major revolution for knowledge and information.

Why will librarians not push EIDOS? You said it will be information users, not librarians, who will be most enthusiastic about EIDOS.

KILGOUR: In the middle of the nineteenth century there were major developments in libraries. In 1843, Jewett developed the structured subject heading index at Brown University. In 1848, Poole indexed periodicals at Yale; in 1873, Melvil Dewey's narrow classification scheme, and 1884 his introduction of the full-time reference librarian.

And that ended it. Except for the introduction of the user-operated photocopy machine in about 1960 at the Harvard Medical Library, there really wasn't any significant change until OCLC came along.

People went into librarianship because it didn't change. It was very stable and innovators weren't attracted to it. But I went into librarianship because I saw an opportunity to innovate.

What will be the characteristics of the user of the library in 1998?

KILGOUR: One of the characteristics is that he or she is going to have to be more satisfied or there aren't going to be libraries, because there will be competition, there certainly will be.

I have a paper out for publication now which reviews about 15 studies, all done in academic libraries (there haven't been any good studies on public libraries) on failure rates. Forty out of one hundred times you don't get what you want from a library and that just is too serious a failure rate.

So you bet it's got to change, for libraries can't go on with that kind of failure. They don't have public support, they get non-support and they complain about it. But who's going to support something that fails nearly half the time?

Does this say that the user is going to become more and more sophisticated in terms of expecting information?

KILGOUR: No. He or she is going to become more and more satisfied. The important thing is that an electronic book is always on the shelf. One hundred people out of one hundred can use it at the same time.

What will save libraries?

KILGOUR: Supplying the information and knowledge that people want when and where they want it. Not just giving them a package and saying, "I hope you'll find what you want in here."

Libraries will be out of business if they don't do a better job of providing answers?

KILGOUR: Yes. I think there's another important thing that's probably going to happen. The reason big libraries exist is because of the historical techniques that are used in a variety of scholarly activities. These techniques are qualitative and require a lot of data. One hundred years ago biology was entirely a qualitative science and its laboratories were natural history museums. Now most of the natural history museums have gone out of being because in the first decade of this century biology shifted from qualitative to quantitative activity, and there was no way that anybody would ever have discovered DNA in a natural history museum. When biology changed entirely so did its research and data sources.

The computer is certainly going to change historical investigation.

Are you saying that all libraries will have to become like the special, corporate library, where either you get the answer or you don't exist?

KILGOUR: That's correct. I've been in librarianship for 50 years and it's been the special librarians, including the medical librarians, who have been the exciting people. In my experience, most of the directors of major research libraries have no understanding of research. They don't understand the scholarly use of their library.

What are the pitfalls to the new technology?

KILGOUR: With OCLC, a lot of things occurred that neither I nor other librarians anticipated. I'll give you one example.

Fifteen years ago, the librarian at Dartmouth and I were having a cup of coffee at an ALA meeting and she said, "Just before I left, my head cataloger came in and said, 'OCLC's created another disaster.'"

I said, "What now?"

And he said, "No more backlog."

Well, this presented a real problem because then he had too many people and this was something that wasn't really anticipated. And there was a lot of this stuff. So the pitfalls are certainly going to be there.

Now let me respond to some of the questions you sent in advance.

What's the best way that I've found to get staff to see a library through the eyes of the user? Be one. Librarians don't use libraries. They don't really use them.

My view on the convergence of libraries and computer centers. That's undesirable. They're going to be doing two totally different things.

Do I see a major influx of high-tech experts? No, I don't see any major influx of high-tech experts. The librarians are going to be different, but they're not going to be high-tech experts.

Beyond the salary level, what do I see as the most significant reason libraries do not attract more of the best and the brightest? Because there's no change and there's no great excitement in librarianship. Innovators still don't go into librarianship. The National Library of Medicine is a major exception; it really has a research and development activity. OCLC and the National Library of Medicine are the two major library research development activities.

Libraries have no statement of purpose. "Service" is not a statement of purpose. The ends that librarians have are to get something off of their desk onto the next desk, and that is not a very fulfilling experience for imaginative people. This has all got to change.

One thing is that librarians are going to have to develop a statement of societal purpose. EIDOS has one, which is that it should contribute to the increase in the welfare and effectiveness of the members of the community. Libraries haven't any statement of purpose like that.

There certainly will be closer working arrangements between librarians and publishers. Let me suggest something. Supposing that OCLC or something like it, some library-oriented organization, does not develop EIDOS. The publishers are much interested in EIDOS and the AAP might develop it. If that happens, librarians are going to become part of the publishing system.

Resource sharing—yes, this is almost certainly going to increase. The last time I saw the figures on OCLC the daily average of interlibrary loan requests was 16,600. That's a daily average. OCLC is increasing the availability of books.

Preservation—I'm not sure that there has to be much preservation. I've got one set that I think I would like to preserve for myself. It's the five volumes of George Sarton's *Introduction to the History of Science*, which is a wonderful resource, but it was printed on terrible paper. Aside from that, I can't think of any more to preserve for myself.

Censorship—I don't think that's important. It generates emotions, but I don't think it's very important.

Budget and fund raising—The only way the library is going to improve its availability of funds is to increase the success that its users have; then it will get more support.

How can a librarian best learn how to become a leader?

KILGOUR: Be one.

You were leading from way back. Something made you a leader. It isn't enough to say, be one. What made you?

KILGOUR: From the start, I have been concerned about improving the availability of information to users. And that has been a life-long professional goal; it still is.

A while back when I was at Harvard I got some of my old professional papers out of the archives and found a memorandum dated 1939 that appointed me to be in charge of increasing the availability of books. The very last sentence, which I'm sure I drafted, gave me responsibility for book availability throughout the whole library. It was signed by both an Assistant Librarian for Reference and Circulation and by me and was addressed to the Director.

I began working in the Harvard Library in October 1934 as a student assistant charging out books at the circulation desk. I got that job through the employment office. I can't remember what I was paid at the beginning, but the year after I graduated, I continued to work in the library, that was 1935–36, and my salary for that year was $960.

The attitude of the people in the circulation department was that those people out front were just a nuisance, and it dawned on me sometime while I was working there that if it weren't for those people, there wouldn't be any circulation department, so I began to try to improve relationships and the feeling of those people about the library.

What I would do was instead of—as happens in most libraries even now—instead of sliding a book across the circulation desk, I would pick it up and hand it to the borrower, who would say, thank you. When I had the bad news that books weren't available—I did a study at Harvard which showed 43% failure—I'd hand the slips to them and tell them the bad news and they'd still say, thank you.

This paid off, because the following June at commencement, a graduate student who had gotten his Ph.D. in history saw me there and came over and said, "I want to tell you about the gratitude that all the graduate students have for the way you've improved that library."

It didn't take very much, but it's an example of how librarians aren't interested in the user, which still happens. Twenty-five years later, I was at the circulation desk at the Yale University

Library, when a fellow came up who looked more or less the way I do right now—well-dressed, white hair—and the clerk at the desk asked, "Are you associated with Yale or are you just an ordinary citizen of New Haven?" And he said he was just an ordinary citizen.

That isn't the way to handle people.

Another time I was in that library on the afternoon of New Year's Eve doing some research myself. There were a couple of borrowers at the circulation desk who were mad as hatters, and one of the young woman attendants in desperation asked me if I could do something.

I said, what's the problem?

Well, they want to take this book out. We're holding it for somebody else. New Year's Day was Friday and the place was going to be closed Saturday and Sunday as well, and it's now the end of the day. The somebody else wouldn't be coming in. So I said, give it to them and charge it until Monday morning.

The staff couldn't do it and their supervisors had taken off so the staff had to stay with the rule.

The same kind of thing happened to me recently in the OSU library. They wouldn't let me take out overnight a book that was in a noncirculating collection just because the rule said so. I pointed out that the real rule was to satisfy the user, but I didn't get the book.

Unfortunately there's an awful lot of this that goes on in libraries. When I first went into librarianship, public librarians used to be called "two-cent tyrants" because, of course, the fine was two cents a day. And as a matter of fact, public libraries, then and now, keep their records on the basis of when a book is due, not who's got the book and when it's going to be available.

Did you have a mentor in the library business?

KILGOUR: Yes. My first professional job was as general assistant to Keyes D. Metcalf, who did a lot for me and supported me in some of my wild ideas. He was a real mentor for four years from '38 to March of '42, when I left to go to war, so to speak, that is, go to OSS.

There's something else about me that's different from most librarians: On my first professional job, I did not have a predecessor. The job was created for me. The next job I had was as Superintendent of Circulation at Harvard Library, a job that had existed before, but since then I've never had a job that wasn't a new job. And half my jobs have been created for me. Most librarians don't have that kind of experience.

When I first was accepted as a freshman at Harvard, I wrote to the student employment office because I had to have a job. The letter I got back asked me not to come to Harvard because I didn't have any financial resources, and their experience was that boys in that situation didn't make it. Therefore, they asked me please not to come, although I had been accepted.

But I was just as stubborn then as I am now—I went.

Afterword

Tomorrow's Library World: Challenges and Opportunities

by Donald E. Riggs

Co-editor Don Riggs puts into context this entire examination of *Libraries in the '90s* and draws from a theoretical framework valuable guides for library leaders. Among the major topics: who and what an "actualized" employee is and his/her expectations of library leadership; why librarians need to learn more about the learning process; how machines will give us time for creativity and innovation; "expert systems" and how they will let reference librarians be more professional; why the future library leader needs to understand the difference between transactional and transformative leadership—and which will work better by the year 2000.

We live in the "rapids of change." The white waters carry us quickly on; we cannot slow down the changes coming to our culture, our society, our families, ourselves. But we do have a choice: we can learn to enjoy turbulence rather than be overwhelmed by it.

—Futurist Robert Theobald

Today is an exciting time to be associated with libraries. The 1990s will be even more eventful for libraries, their users, and the people working in them. Positive changes are occurring at a rate faster than ever before in the history of libraries in the U.S.

It was 31 years after the first permanent English settlement in America was started at Jamestown in 1607, when the first U.S. library (at Harvard College) was founded. One of the nation's first free tax-supported public libraries was established in Peterborough, NH, in 1833. The free public library concept was nurtured by steel magnate Andrew Carnegie by his series of gifts between 1881 and 1919, during which time he helped build 2,500 libraries in the English-speaking world (about 1,700 of them in the U.S.).

Changes occurred slowly in the U.S. and international library worlds. It was not until the 1960s that dramatic changes began taking place in libraries. Obviously, the use of computers provided the chief impetus for this change. The advent of the computer in the library world jolted many librarians; however, when it was realized that the machine was only a tool for improving library service, a more positive attitude displaced baseless apprehensions about the new technology.

FACTORS AFFECTING LIBRARIES

The 1990s will bring many changes that will have a direct impact on libraries and their services. Some of these factors can be predicted with some degree of accuracy, while others remain nebulous. The U.S. Bureau of the Census projects that by the year 2000 the U.S. will have a population of about 268 million. This projection may be too low due to larger than anticipated immigration from Latin American and Third World countries. Population shifts from one geographical area to another and the steady heavy immigration of Latin Americans will have a direct bearing on the service levels provided by some public libraries.

In the 1990s, we will have more people above 65 years of age than ever before, and more people in this age group will be in the workforce. Conversely, the number of people under 18 years of age is expected to decline by 2000. What impact the larger number of older persons will have on libraries is yet to be seen.

The nature of work will continue to change. Greater emphasis will be given to the service and information economy in the '90s. Today's typical worker moves, handles, and transfers—and even occasionally analyzes and interprets—information as opposed to minerals and auto parts. Yet the '90s may not generate any extraordinary demands for new skills. Computer technology may appear to us—the first generation of observers and participants— as a promising (or threatening) revolutionary transformation of work and society. It does not follow, however, that users will have to be familiar with the mysteries of computer technology. We know how to operate a telephone, but very few of us fathom the technology that makes it work. Whatever wonders computer technology may spawn, the production managers will simplify the work.

Less than a decade ago, few people could locate the "on" switch of an IBM PC. Today, "user friendly" computers require only marginal changes in skill requirements. Actually, the user of personal computers and information appliances can expect to find them easier to utilize in the near future. The ideal situation should provide the user the opportunity to get "online" as easily as shifting one's car from "park" to "drive." Workers who spend time in the online environment readily see the advantages of using computers in libraries, and they tend to expect libraries to have modern technology in place (e.g., an online catalog).

At the top of Maslow's well-known ladder of basic human needs, one finds self-actualization. Achieving the top rung of Maslow's ladder is a matter of developing the inner nature or the potential we each have within us. Executives and mailroom clerks alike question the way in which they spend their time at work. A key management issue in the '90s will be these workers' increasing need for self-actualization.

Libraries will have to be proactive in accommodating the actualized employee. Self-actualization means a healthy personality, wholeness, a full-functioning being, and psychological "completion." The actualized person is creative, independent, and self-sufficient. These individuals will increasingly have as their primary focus personal goals, inner values, and the creation of distinct lifestyles. (1) More and more workers are saying that money is not everything. Employers will have to find innovative ways in the '90s to attract the new "actualized" workers, whose values of personal development make them desirable, but difficult, to retain.

NEW APPROACHES TO LEARNING

Psychologists define learning as the process by which changes in behavior result from experience or practice. No one has and probably no one ever fully will understand how learning really takes place. Nevertheless, we can expect greater attention will be given to the learning process as we move into the next century.

Librarians will have to possess a better understanding of the various learning processes in order to serve users more effectively. Library schools normally do not offer a course in learning behaviors/processes; therefore, special provision needs to be made to correct this deficiency for all librarians working with users. Formal classes or well-structured workshops may fill the bill.

It is estimated that the total knowledge of humanity now doubles every seven years. And it is not only the amount of information that has grown. The speed of its processing (1.2 billion operations per second in a Cray 2 computer), the storage capacity (the equivalent of 275,000 pages on a compact laser disk), and the ease and rapidity of access through telematics have totally transformed the servicing of knowledge. (2)

The transformation of our society from a civilization based on raw materials, capital, and production to one based on human resources and knowledge is an irreversible development, with huge consequences for our learning systems. Getting a working knowledge of the theories and practices of learning will repay librarians many times.

CREATIVITY

Advances in technology will make it possible someday soon for human beings to spend more time creating. Isaac Asimov believes that during the early part of the twenty-first century, "Machines will do the humdrum work of humanity. The computers will keep the world going, and human beings will be free at last to do things that only human beings can do—to create." (3)

Innovation, an aspect of creativity, comes slowly in libraries. There is little latitude for being an innovative librarian. However, technology developments in the '90s will provide more opportunity for innovation in libraries. Herbert White believes that what senior library managers can and should do is to provide a climate that welcomes and encourages innovators and entrepreneurs, that protects them from second-guessers when they fail, that guards them in their "difference" from colleagues and coworkers, and that makes it clear that risk is welcome even when it leads to failure, and is still preferable to never trying or suggesting anything. (4)

Asimov goes on to say, "The work of the future will be creation, done by each in one's own fashion. People will judge you not by how long you work or how many routine units you turn out, but rather by how much you increase the joy of the world. They will want to know how much of what you do gives pleasure not only to yourself, but to others. How much is useful. That is what will count." (5)

Library managers can foster creativity in their staffs by better understanding what makes creative people tick. Creative people draw ideas from almost any source and recognize interrelationships and parallels that may be appropriately transferred. Seemingly unrelated things may be combined by creative association. James Watt's tea kettle opened the door to the steam engine, and everyone has heard how a falling apple helped Newton get to the core of the law of gravity.

INTELLIGENT MACHINES

Over the past 10 years libraries have witnessed the online revolution. Circulation control, reserve, acquisitions, serials, and the public access catalog have all been placed online. What's the next step toward improving services via technology? Loading bibliographic, numeric, and public research databases onto the public access catalog is a good one for a starter.

The next phenomenon that will make a dramatic impact on the work of librarians is expert systems. In a nutshell, an expert system is an intelligent computer program that uses knowledge and inference procedures to solve problems that are difficult enough to require significant human expertise for their solutions. The library expert systems currently in design or implementation stage can be used on microcomputers. It is important to remember that an expert system is a subset of artificial intelligence, and that it has to rival the human system if it is to be a genuine expert system. If library applications of expert systems are to function like a human expert, then they must be able to do things human experts do. They must be able to ask questions, solve problems, explain their reasoning, and justify their conclusions.

Experiments with expert systems in libraries began in the late 1970s. There are only a handful of library expert systems in existence today. Applications can be found in cataloging, reference, and management. Other expert systems are in the developmental stage and will be introduced in libraries in the early '90s.

One of the difficulties of expert systems is the control of a knowledge domain. If it is to be a true expert system, it must be able to answer all questions, for example, pertaining to a given subject matter. Many reference questions tend to be repeated, and many of the questions are "ready reference" or directional in nature. Following are some advantages an expert system could provide in reference service:

1. Service can be provided throughout the library, not just at the reference desk. Expert systems on microcomputers can be located at convenient locations for the users. If the user is on the fifth level of the library and needs an answer to a question, a conveniently located expert system can save a trip back to the first level to consult with the reference desk.
2. Subject specialists have expert knowledge that is not held by other reference librarians. An expert system can capture this special knowledge and make it available to the library user when the subject specialist is not in the library.
3. General or specialized service can be provided after all librarians have gone home for the evening. In most libraries, reference librarians leave their posts around 10 p.m., but the library may remain open until 2 a.m. Expert systems do not experience fatigue.
4. Many users can be accommodated at the same time. The average number of reference librarians available at the reference counter/desk is two or three, while 20 to 30 expert system terminals can be made available for users. This eliminates the frustration of waiting in line for assistance from a librarian.
5. Bibliographic instruction can be provided by an expert system. This service is very important, but it can become boring when the librarian has to repeat it.

Expert systems will not replace librarians. They will enable librarians to engage in more professional work. OCLC did not replace catalogers, and it will not do so. It reduced the need for staff in some cataloging areas. Expert systems will provide better library service in a more cost-effective manner.

All of the technology used in libraries up to the present time has consisted of machines that we have had to "talk down" to; expert systems offer the first machines that can "converse intelligently" with us. Expert systems will also provide an intelligent front-end mechanism for a user-friendly interface to other library software packages.

COLLECTIONS AND ONLINE ACCESS

Undoubtedly, the collection format of our nation's libraries will remain basically as is during the '90s. Books and periodicals in paper copy will continue to be the primary carriers of knowledge. We will witness a conversion to electronic formats for periodicals; 15 to 20% of the scientific periodicals may be in electronic format (full-text online) by the mid '90s.

Librarians and other persons (e.g., city managers, college presidents) responsible for libraries have little say about the format in which items are published. Publishers, driven by the profit motive, have essentially made the decisions regarding how and when items will be published. Will this change in the future? It may, depending on how effective concerned librarians and others responsible for libraries can organize themselves to work with or against, if necessary, publishing firms.

Most publishing firms are sensitive to keeping prices down and working cooperatively with libraries. However, a few publishers of some major scientific periodicals have not made an effort to hold prices within the reach of libraries. Some periodicals' subscription prices have increased more than 50% in one year. Such gigantic price increases cannot be tolerated by libraries.

Libraries are faced with a double bind: The value of the U.S. dollar has fallen drastically in the foreign market while concurrently foreign publishers have increased periodicals' prices beyond what U.S. libraries can afford. If the foreign publishers do not make financial allowances for U.S. libraries, then we will likely see a concerted effort by academic and special libraries to seek alternatives in order to gain the knowledge carried in the periodicals in question. Alternate ways could include contracting with university presses to publish more scientific periodicals, or having the periodicals purchased by only a few libraries and providing the required periodical articles via interlibrary loan using next-day telefacsimile transmission. One thing is certain: The current practice of a few publishers raising annual subscriptions by astronomical rates will not be condoned by libraries in the '90s.

The online catalog provides many conveniences for users. For example, many online catalogs permit users to dial-in from their modem-equipped personal computers. Users then have bibliographic access to the library's holdings from the office, dormitory, and home. By the mid '90s the online catalog will be common in most libraries, and by the year 2000 the card catalog will be archaic. Pressure from users will bring forth necessary funding for libraries to convert the card catalog records into electronic format. Users can expect to find the online catalog carrying more than bibliographic records for books and periodicals. Various databases will also be mounted on the online catalog.

VALUE-ADDED SERVICES

Many large libraries do not have sufficient staff to work with users in finding the information they need. In many large academic and public libraries, librarians can only give "possible" sources for locating the desired information. For example, if a user poses the question—"How many planetariums were constructed in the U.S. in 1985?"—the overworked reference librarian will probably tell the user two or three sources in which the answer may be found.

Since time is also equated to money, many users are happy to pay a fee for the information they are seeking. Large libraries with a huge number of users and insufficient librarians are developing mechanisms that allow users to pay for such information.

Libraries are providing such value-added services on a daily basis. Implementation of the online catalog, for example, permits many more users at any given time to have access to the library's bibliographic records. Card catalogs can only be used by coming to the library; the online catalog will permit access from anywhere (homes, offices) via a modem-equipped terminal.

"Value-added" will be a common term used by libraries and their users in the '90s. Private firms will most likely try to capitalize on the provision of information for a price. How much competition they will present libraries remains unknown.

TRANSFORMATIVE LEADERSHIP

For some unknown reasons, persons holding responsible positions in libraries have done little to articulate the importance of leadership. Most of the discussions at conferences and the professional literature have focused on management practices. A quick check of the themes of American Library Association presidents reveals that Margaret Chisholm (1987–88 ALA President) was the first to use "leadership" as the annual theme in the 112-year history of the organization. Good management is honorable, but our libraries require more than just day-by-day management. They must have a clearly defined mission, a common vision of their future, and a dynamic action plan.

The type of library leadership required in the '90s and beyond will not be that of a transactional nature. Again, day-to-day transactions are important and must be completed, but a dependence on transactional leadership only is dangerous. Thriving libraries in the '90s will demand transformative leadership.

Warren Bennis describes transformative leadership as the capacity to translate intentions into reality and sustain it. This type of leadership can move organizations from current to future states, create visions of potential opportunities for organizations, instill within employees commitment to change, and instill within organizations new cultures and strategies that mobilize and focus energy and resources. (6) Transformative leadership is more complex and potent than transactional leadership. It is dynamic in the sense that leaders throw themselves into a relationship with followers who become "elevated" by it and often become more active themselves, thereby creating new cadres of leaders in the library.

Transforming leaders like to make things happen; they arouse confidence in followers, and consequently, the followers have more enthusiasm and confidence in attaining their library's goals. An infusion of new values in libraries will occur under transformative leadership. A transforming leader believes in staying ahead of the changing library environment, thinks that maintaining the status quo is too risky, and promotes the entrepreneurial spirit. While the transacting leader focuses on task-motivation, the transforming leader identifies relationship-motivation as a major target. Staff are encouraged by the transforming leader to reach for higher, more innovative levels of achievement. More compassion for the staff is expressed by the transforming leader.

During the next decade we will see more evidence of transformative leadership in libraries. If libraries are to survive and thrive, they will need more than good management and transactional leadership. The future for libraries is bright, but libraries will have more than their share of growing pains.

Bennis firmly believes that most organizations are managed, not led. He also believes that organizations lacking transformative leadership will have a tough time surviving the '90s. (7) One can also apply this line of reasoning to the "health and well being" of our libraries during the next decade. Will our libraries be led, or will they struggle to survive?

STRATEGIC THINKING

Nearly every aspect of a library will undergo some change in the '90s. Many of the changes will occur in a manner that will cause the library to be reactive. Library staffs will continue to be overburdened with their regular daily duties and they will not have much time to contemplate the future. However, the pace of change in libraries will continue to accelerate.

Strategic thinking about how to plan for and create the library's future is of critical importance. This type of thinking will not be limited only to the library's leaders and managers, but all professional staff will be required to participate. Strategic thinking may result in a strategic plan or some other type of strategic management tool, but the crux of the matter remains "thinking strategically."

Peter Davis elaborates on the importance of strategic thinking:

> In the placid world of traditional librarianship, strategic thinking was an unnecessary and indeed alien idea connoting conniving in its worst extreme. The library was meant to be carried wherever the satisfaction of the user needs took it. In the turbulent, resource scarce environment of contemporary librarianship, strategic thinking becomes indispensable. However, most librarians are simply not practiced in strategic thinking, which requires a shift in mind set. A mind which is used to thinking forward from action to consequences, must begin to focus on "backward analysis" from desirable future outcomes to immediate requirements. Capability to think strategically needs to be developed in most managers; unfortunately, it seldom is. (8)

According to the proverb, where there is no vision, the people will perish. A vision of a library's future is paramount. The creation of this vision cannot be done by the library director only; it must involve several key participants within and outside of the library. The "think tank" approach can be used effectively in re-examining the mission statement of the library. It is the responsibility of the library director to express the importance of the "think tank" groups, and to articulate that they are not just another library committee.

Naturally, the strategic thinking process is an intellectual activity. It should involve the principles of critical thinking. The '90s will require that more critical thought be given to the external environment of the library. The library should be prepared, based on strategic thinking, to capitalize on, offset, or cope with significant external forces.

Sun Tzu, second century B.C. Chinese philosopher, said: "What enables a person to achieve far greater than ordinary persons is foreknowledge." Strategic thinking, or foreknowledge, about libraries in the '90s will be a great providence.

REFERENCES

1. Marsha Sinetar, "The Actualized Worker," *Futurist* 21 (March–April 1987): 21–25.

2. Mahdi Elmandjra, "Learning Needs in a Changing World," *Futurist* 21 (March–April 1987): 60.

3. Isaac Asimov, "The Permanent Dark Age: Can We Avoid It?" in *Working in the Twenty-First Century*, ed. C. Stewart Sheppard and Donald C. Carroll (New York: John Wiley, 1980), p. 10.

4. Herbert S. White, "Entrepreneurship and the Library Profession," *Journal of Library Administration* 8 (Spring 1987): 11-27.

5. Asimov, p. 10.

6. Warren Bennis and Burt Nanus, *Leaders: The Strategies for Taking Charge* (New York: Harper & Row, 1985), p. 17.

7. Bennis and Nanus, p. 218.

8. Peter Davis, "Libraries at the Turning Point: Issues in Proactive Planning," *Journal of Library Administration* 12 (Summer 1980): 11-24.

Subject Index

———— ◆◆◆ ————

Name Index

———— ◆ ◆ ◆ ————

www.ingramcontent.com/pod-product-compliance
Ingram Content Group UK Ltd.
Pitfield, Milton Keynes, MK11 3LW, UK
UKHW020738280225
455688UK00012B/719